D1608753

# Tapestry

**William K. Durr**
**Jean M. LePere**
**Bess Niehaus**
**Barbara York**

CONSULTANT Paul McKee

HOUGHTON MIFFLIN COMPANY • Boston

Atlanta • Dallas • Geneva, Illinois • Hopewell, New Jersey • Palo Alto • Toronto

# Acknowledgments

For each of the selections listed below, grateful acknowledgment is made for permission to adapt and/or reprint copyrighted material, as follows:

"Anyone Could, But." From *Act It Out* by Bernice Wells Carlson. Copyright © 1956 by Pierce and Washabaugh. Used by permission of Abingdon Press.

*Bascombe, the Fastest Hound Alive* by George Goodman is adapted by permission of William Morrow & Company, Inc. Copyright © 1958 by George Goodman.

"Benjy and the Barking Bird." Adapted from *Benjy and the Barking Bird* by Margaret Bloy Graham. Copyright © 1971 by Margaret Bloy Graham. Reprinted by permission of Harper & Row, Publishers, Inc.

"The Big Pile of Dirt." Adaptation of *The Big Pile of Dirt* by Eleanor Clymer. Copyright © 1968 by Eleanor Clymer. Reprinted by permission of Holt, Rinehart and Winston, Inc.

"Butterfly, butterfly," reprinted from *Music of Acoma, Isleta, Cochiti and Zuni Pueblos* by Frances Densmore, the *Bureau of American Ethnology, Bulletin 165.* Used with permission of the Smithsonian Institution Press.

"Child of the Navajos," reprinted by permission of Dodd, Mead & Company, Inc. from *Child of the Navajos* by Seymour Reit and Paul Conklin. Copyright © 1971 by Seymour Reit. Copyright © 1971 by Paul Conklin.

*Down, Down the Mountain* by Ellis Credle. Reprinted by permission of Thomas Nelson Inc. Copyright © 1934, 1961 by Ellis Credle.

"Evan's Corner." Adapted from *Evan's Corner* by Elizabeth Starr Hill. Text copyright © 1967 by Elizabeth Starr Hill. Illustrations copyright © 1967 by Nancy Grossman. Reprinted by permission of Holt, Rinehart and Winston, Inc. and Brandt . & Brandt.

*Fidelia* by Ruth Adams. Adapted by permission of Lothrop, Lee & Shepard Co., Inc. Copyright © 1970 by Ruth Adams.

"Josefina February." Reprinted by permission of Charles Scribner's Sons from *Josefina February* by Evaline Ness. Copyright © 1963 by Evaline Ness.

"The Little Boy's Secret" by David L. Harrison. Reprinted with permission from *The Book of Giant Stories* by David L. Harrison. 1972. Illustrations © by Philippe Fix. Published by McGraw-Hill Book Company. Adapted from the original by permission of Jonathan Cape Limited.

"A Little Yellow Cricket," from *Singing for Power: The Song Magic of the Papago Indians of Southern Arizona* by Ruth Murry Underhill. Originally published by the University of California Press; reprinted by permission of The Regents of the University of California.

"Lyle," from *Bronzeville Boys and Girls* by Gwendolyn Brooks. Text copyright © 1956 by Gwendolyn Brooks

Blakely. Reprinted by permission of Harper & Row, Publishers, Inc.

"Ma Lien and the Magic Brush." Adaptation of *Ma Lien and the Magic Brush* by Hisako Kimishima. Illustrated by Kei Wakana. English version by Alvin Tresselt. Text copyright © 1968 by Parents' Magazine Press. Used by permission of Parents' Magazine Press.

"My Kitten," from *Feathered Ones and Furry* by Aileen Fisher. Copyright © 1971 by Aileen Fisher, with permission of Thomas Y. Crowell Company, Inc., publisher.

"Pip Squeak, Mouse in Shining Armor." Copyright © 1971 by Robert Kraus. Adapted from *Pip Squeak, Mouse in Shining Armor* by Robert Kraus, by permission of Windmill Books, an Intext publisher.

"Rain Poem" by Elizabeth Coatsworth. Reprinted with permission of The Macmillan Company from *Poems* by Elizabeth Coatsworth. © by The Macmillan Company 1957.

"Riddles," from *Beginning-To-Read Riddles and Jokes* by Alice Thompson Gilbreath. Published by Follett Publishing Company, © 1967. Used by permission.

"Rufty and Tufty," by Isabell Hempseed. Reprinted with permission of Evans Brothers, Ltd. from *A Book of a Thousand Poems.* © by Evans Brothers, Ltd.

"Saturday Surprise," by Jean Fritz. From *Round About the City* by Child Study Association. Copyright © 1966 by Thomas Y. Crowell Company, Inc., with permission of the publisher.

"Sound of Water," by Mary O'Neill. Text copyright © 1966 by Mary O'Neill. From *What Is That Sound!* Used by permission of Atheneum Publishers.

"Spring Wind," by Charlotte Zolotow. Copyright © 1970, text by Charlotte Zolotow, pictures by Regina Shekerjian. Reprinted from *River Winding* by Charlotte Zolotow, by permission of Abelard-Schuman Limited, an Intext publisher.

"Sunning," from *Crickety Cricket! The Best Loved Poems of James S. Tippett.* Text copyright © 1973 by Martha K. Tippett. Reprinted by permission of Harper & Row, Publisher, Inc. British rights granted by World's Work Ltd.

"Turtles," from *Town and Countryside Poems.* Copyright © 1968 by John Travers Moore. Reprinted with permission of Albert Whitman & Company, Chicago, Ill.

"Who's In Holes?" From *Who's In Holes?* by Richard Armour. Copyright © 1971 by Richard Armour and Paul Galdone. Used with permission of McGraw-Hill Book Co. British rights granted by World's Work Ltd.

*Illustrators:* PP. 7–23, MARGARET BLOY GRAHAM; PP. 24–32, KINUKO CRAFT; P. 33, ANNE PHILBRICK HALL; PP. 34–51, ANGELA ADAMS; PP. 52–53, ED EMBERLY; P. 54, EVELYN MARCUS; PP. 55–65, PHILIPPE FIX; PP. 66–68, ED EMBERLY; P. 69, MARY AUSTIN; PP. 71–96, TRUE KELLY; PP. 99–123, KEVIN CALLAHAN; PP. 124–126, ED EMBERLY; P. 127, LADY McCRADY; PP. 128–129, REBECCA BAXTER; PP. 130–145, SUSAN SWANN; PP. 146–148, ED EMBERLY; PP. 153–184, NANCY GROSSMAN; P. 185, DOROTHEA SIERRA; P. 186, BILL CHARMATZ; PP. 187–200, IMERO GOBBATO; PP. 203–224, LINDA BOEHM; P. 225, SUSAN ANDERSON; PP. 226–227, ED EMBERLY; PP. 234–251, KEI WAKANA; P. 252, LYNN TITLEMAN; PP. 253–277, GARY FUJIWARA (Design and Illustration); PP. 278–281, ED EMBERLY; PP. 283–312, ALFRED OLSCHEWSKI.

*Photographers:* PP. 70, 127, WALTER CHANDOHA; PP. 149–152, BONNIE UNSWORTH; PP. 228–233, WERNER STOY, CAMERA HAWAII, INC.; PP. 253–277, PAUL CONKLIN.

*Book cover, title page, and magazine covers, PP. 5, 201, SUSAN ANDERSON; magazine cover, P. 97, CHRIS CZERNOTA.*

Copyright © 1976 by Houghton Mifflin Company
All rights reserved. No part of this work may be reproduced or transmitted in any form or by any means, electronic or mechanical, including photocopying and recording, or by any information storage or retrieval system, without permission in writing from the publisher.
PRINTED IN THE U.S.A.

ISBN: 0-395-20409-7

# Contents

# Secrets and Surprises

# Secrets and Surprises

# Benjy and the Barking Bird

by Margaret Bloy Graham

Benjy was a brown dog with long ears and a short tail. He loved everybody in his family — Mother, Father, Linda, and Jimmy — and they all loved him.

He was a happy dog until he heard the words, "Tomorrow Aunt Sarah is coming for a visit, and she's bringing Tilly."

Tilly was Aunt Sarah's parrot. When Tilly was there, Benjy's family always fussed over her and never gave him any attention. That made Benjy jealous.

The minute Aunt Sarah got there, she said,
"Come on, Tilly, show them your new trick.
Say *bow-wow,* sweetie."

"BOW-WOW! BOW-WOW!" squawked Tilly.

"Hey," said Jimmy, "Tilly can bark better
than Benjy."

Benjy couldn't stand it. He went out
into the backyard. He decided not to come
into the house again until that awful parrot
had gone. He could still hear her: "BOW-WOW!
BOW-WOW! BOW-WOW!"

Tilly barked so long and so loud that all the
dogs in the neighborhood came running. Soon
the backyard was full of barking dogs. They
made so much noise that Benjy's ears hurt.
Father came to the door and shouted, "Get out
of here!"

"Be quiet, Tilly!" said Aunt Sarah. "I don't
know what's got into that bird. She's been a
problem all spring."

"Linda, dear," said Mother, "put Tilly
up in Aunt Sarah's room so we can have peace
and quiet for lunch."

Benjy was still outside, more jealous than
ever. Suddenly he had an idea. While the family
was having lunch, he sneaked into the house,
past the dining room, and up to Aunt Sarah's
room. Tilly was asleep, tired out from her
barking.

Carefully Benjy picked up her cage and
brought it out into the backyard. He was just
lifting it into the trash can when the cage door
hit the side. The door came open and Tilly
escaped!

Off she flew to the big maple tree where there
were a lot of sparrows. In a flash Tilly and the
sparrows flew away.

Benjy just stood there . . . .

Then all at once he felt happy. Tilly was
gone!

Quickly he hid the cage in the trash can and
ran into the house.

After lunch Aunt Sarah went to her room.
Right away she ran out screaming, "Tilly's gone!"

Everyone began talking at once: "Impossible!"
"No!" "Where did she go?"

Finally Father said, "Don't worry. We'll
find her."

So the whole family set out to look for Tilly,
all except Aunt Sarah. She was too upset to go.
Benjy was watching her. He'd been so happy
that Tilly was gone — now he felt awful.
He'd rather have her back.

Maybe she *had* come back. He ran
to the maple tree, but no Tilly. He looked
for her everywhere, but no Tilly. All he
could see were a few sparrows flying
around the roof of the house.

Meanwhile the family searched for Tilly
all over town, but they could not find her.

"It's getting late," Father said finally.
"Let's go home. We'll put an ad in the paper
tonight. Tomorrow we'll start out early and
take Benjy with us."

## A Real Bird Dog

Next morning when everyone was having breakfast, Benjy ran in barking excitedly.

"Stop it, Benjy," said Mother. "You'll remind Aunt Sarah of Tilly."

But Benjy kept on barking. Then he ran up the stairs.

"Go and see what he's up to, children," said Father.

The children ran after Benjy. "Father! Mother!" they called from the attic. "Come quick!"

Father, Mother, and Aunt Sarah dashed up
to the attic. There was Benjy barking
at the window — and there was Tilly right
outside! She was flying around with a twig
in her beak.

"Tilly," cried Aunt Sarah. "What *are*
you doing?"

"She's helping a sparrow build a nest,"
said Linda. "That's what birds do in the spring."

"She never did *that* before," said Aunt Sarah.
"Tilly, please come in." Aunt Sarah tried and
tried to get Tilly to come inside.

But it was no use. Tilly paid no attention.
She and the sparrow kept bringing more and
more twigs and pieces of string. There was now
a big nest just above the attic window.

"We'll have to ask the Fire Department
to catch Tilly," said Father.

In all the excitement nobody noticed
that Benjy had left.

An hour later the phone rang.

It was Mr. Jones, the man from the pet store. "Your little dog is here," he said, "and he won't go home."

"I'll send the children to get him," said Father.

When Linda and Jimmy got to the pet store, there was Benjy, staring up at a parrot.

"I don't know why," said Mr. Jones, "but he keeps looking at Sparky. He seems to want that parrot."

"I bet I know why Benjy wants him," said Jimmy.

"Me too," said Linda. "Please, Mr. Jones, let us take Sparky home."

Meanwhile the ladder truck of the Fire Department had come. The ladder was being raised to the attic window.

A fire fighter with a net climbed up. "Here, Tilly! Here, Tilly!" he called.

The grown-ups watched eagerly. No one had noticed that the children were back with Benjy and Sparky — no one, that is, except Tilly. From the roof she headed straight for Sparky's cage, sat in front of it, and cooed and cooed. It was love at first sight!

Linda opened the cage door and Tilly flew
right in.

"Why, Tilly's been lonely," said Aunt Sarah.
"I never thought of that.  How wonderful you
children were to get her a friend!"

"That was Benjy's idea," said Jimmy.

Then everyone began talking at once: "What
a dog!" "How clever he is!" "A real bird dog!"

Benjy just stood there wagging his tail.

Next spring when Aunt Sarah came for a visit,
she came alone. "I left Tilly and Sparky
with a bird-sitter," she said. "They're so
happy together. And just think, Benjy's the one
who started it all."

This time Benjy really enjoyed Aunt Sarah's visit. She took him for a walk every day and always got him something special.

And from then on, Benjy was Aunt Sarah's favorite dog, and Aunt Sarah was Benjy's favorite aunt.

The End

# Anyone Could, But
## by Bernice Wells Carlson

People in the Play

LORD CHAMBERLAIN        TWO WOMEN

KING        TWO MEN

TWO SHEPHERDS        GREG

**Time:** One day long ago

**Place:** A road. A stone is in the road. The Lord Chamberlain and the King stand on either side of the stone.

LORD CHAMBERLAIN: Your Highness, I do not understand. Why did you dig a hole in the middle of the road? You put a pot of gold in the hole. And then you put this huge stone over the gold! The stone is in the way.

KING: Yes, it is. But this stone may help me find someone.

LORD CHAMBERLAIN:   Your Highness, you'll
never catch a thief this way.  A thief
will never look for gold down there.

KING:   I'm not looking for a thief.  I don't think
anyone will find the gold down there.
But someone may.

LORD CHAMBERLAIN:   Your Highness, are you
feeling well?  Is your head all right?
What is the matter?

KING:   Don't worry, Lord Chamberlain.
My head is well.  My heart is heavy.
You see, I am worried about my people.

LORD CHAMBERLAIN:   I can understand that.
They bring you every little problem they have.

KING:   That's true.

LORD CHAMBERLAIN:   They depend on you
for everything.

KING:   That's just the trouble.  They
depend upon me too much.
I think they have forgotten
how to help themselves.
I think they have forgotten
how to help one another.

LORD CHAMBERLAIN:   But what good is a stone
in the road?

KING:   You'll see.  Shh!  Here come two
shepherds.  Let's hide.  *(They leave.)*

FIRST SHEPHERD:   Just look at that!  A stone in the road!

SECOND SHEPHERD:   Of all things!  I'm certainly glad it wasn't there this morning!

FIRST SHEPHERD:   That's right.  The sheep would have had to go around.

SECOND SHEPHERD:   I hope someone tells the king about this.

FIRST SHEPHERD:   I hope he gets it out of the way, and fast!  *(Shepherds leave. King and Lord Chamberlain come back.)*

27

KING: See what I mean?

LORD CHAMBERLAIN: I think so. Shh! Here come two women. *(Lord Chamberlain and King leave. Two women come in.)*

FIRST WOMAN: Well, look at that!

SECOND WOMAN: What a terrible stone in the road!

FIRST WOMAN: I'm glad it isn't dark. I might have stumbled on it.

SECOND WOMAN: You might do worse than that. What is this world coming to? A stone in the road! Where is the king? *(Women leave.)*

**FIRST MAN:** *(Coming in with Second Man.)*
Yes, business was good, very good. Look!
What is this? A stone in the road.

**SECOND MAN:** Something should be done
at once!

**FIRST MAN:** That stone will get in people's way
and hurt our business.

**SECOND MAN:** I wonder if the king knows
about this.

**FIRST MAN:** The king must be slipping,
letting a stone stay in the middle
of the road. *(Men leave.)*

GREG: *(Coming in whistling.)* Wow!

Look at that stone! Right in the middle
of the road. Lucky I saw it before it got dark.
Someone might have bumped into it and
been hurt. Wonder if I can move it.
Let's see. If I push here, it will roll
down there. Nothing's in the way.
*(Pushes stone.)* There! There it goes!
*(Looks down.)* Hey! What's in the hole?
Gold! It must be the king's gold. No one else
has that much gold! Wonder if someone
stole it. I must tell the king. What will
I do? I can't carry it all. I must get help.

KING: *(Coming in.)* Wait, lad. I've been
looking for you.

GREG: Oh, Your Highness, I just found
this gold. I didn't steal it. Really,
I didn't. There was a stone here.
I rolled it away. Believe me, sir!

KING:   I believe you, lad, because I saw
it all.  I planned it all.

GREG:   You planned it all?

KING:   Yes, I have been looking for someone
in my land who thinks of others.
I have been looking for someone
who can do things for himself.
I waited all day, lad.  But at last
I found you.

GREG:   All day, sir?  Why, anyone
could move that stone.

KING:   Anyone could do it, but only you
did do it.  Thank you, lad.  The gold
is yours.

# rain poem

The rain was like a little mouse,
quiet, small and gray.
It pattered all around the house
and then it went away.

It did not come, I understand,
indoors at all, until
it found an open window and
left tracks across the sill.

*Elizabeth Coatsworth*

# Saturday Surprise

*by Jean Fritz*

As soon as Peggy woke up, she smiled. The sun was shining. It was just the day to go around the world.

Every Saturday Uncle Charlie took Peggy on a surprise trip.

Once he took her to a bench in the sky. When she looked down, she looked way, way down. At the bottom there were people playing football.

Another time Uncle Charlie took her to the moon.
The moon was on the ceiling of a big room. And the
stars were there, too. Peggy held her head back so long
her neck hurt.

Today Peggy and Uncle Charlie were going around the world. Peggy jumped out of bed and started to dress.

Just then her mother came in. "Peggy," she said, "I have some bad news."

Peggy had one shoe on and one shoe off.

"Uncle Charlie just called. He can't go with you. He has to go out of town," her mother said.

"Well, he can't!" Peggy stamped her foot. "He has to take me around the world."

Then she thought a minute. "How do you go around the world?"

"In a boat. Uncle Charlie was going to take you in a boat all around the city. He'll do it another time," her mother said.

Peggy knew, of course, that she couldn't go in a boat all by herself. She knew her mother couldn't take her because her mother worked on Saturday. And there was no one else. Peggy and her mother lived alone.

Peggy stamped her foot again.

"I'm sorry," her mother said. "But, anyway, Uncle Charlie has found someone to take you to the park."

"Who?"

"A lady named Miss Finney," said her mother.

"A stranger!" Peggy cried.

"She's a friend of Uncle Charlie's," her mother said.

"Well, she's not *my* friend. She's a stranger." Peggy threw herself across her bed. She didn't like strangers.

"I'm sure Miss Finney is nice," Peggy's mother said.

Peggy was sure she wasn't.  She knew just what Miss
Finney would be like.  She would be tall and thin and
cross.  She would wear black pinchy shoes, and she'd
sit on a park bench.  She wouldn't go any place.  She'd
just sit and sit.

When the doorbell rang, Peggy and her mother went
to the door.  But Peggy wouldn't talk to Miss Finney.
She wouldn't look at her.

Of course, she couldn't help seeing the shoes.  They
were black and pinchy.

Well, she wouldn't even walk with Miss Finney.

When they went out, Peggy walked two steps behind her. Peggy kept her eyes down and followed the black, pinchy shoes.

At the corner they passed a police officer. He was a friend of Peggy's.

"Hi, Peggy," he said. "Where are you going *this* Saturday?"

"No place," Peggy said.

At the next corner they passed the candy-store man.

"Where are you going today, Peggy?" he asked.

"No place," said Peggy.

The black pinchy shoes stopped. They turned. They pointed at the candy-store man.

"We're going visiting," Miss Finney said. "Peggy and I are going to the park and visit some of my friends."

"More strangers!" Peggy thought. "A whole day of strangers!" Well, she wasn't going to look at any of them.

But when they got to the park, Miss Finney didn't speak to any strangers. She didn't stop at any benches. She didn't even stay on the path. She walked right across the grass and under the trees.

It was hard for Peggy to follow the black, pinchy shoes. She could hardly see where she was going. Then suddenly, she found herself at the edge of a pond. The black, pinchy shoes stopped.

## Strangers — Friends

"Good morning, Hortense," Miss Finney said. "Peggy and I have brought you some breakfast."

Before she knew what she was doing, Peggy looked up. There was a white swan. It was swimming toward her. And there was Miss Finney. She was tall but she wasn't cross looking.

"Hortense is one of my friends," said Miss Finney. She reached into her handbag and pulled out some bread. "If you'd like, you may feed Hortense," she said. "You can break this up for her."

Peggy threw pieces of bread on the water. She watched as Hortense bent her long, long neck down to eat them.

When the bread was gone, Miss Finney said they were going across the park to visit another friend.

"If he's there," Miss Finney said. "Sometimes he has to go downtown on a job."

This time when Peggy followed Miss Finney, she didn't look at the black, pinchy shoes. She looked up at her. And she wondered who the next friend would be. But she didn't ask.

After a while Miss Finney pointed. "There he is," she said. "Under that tree."

Parked on the side of the road was a shiny black carriage. In front of the carriage, there was a shiny black horse.

"That's Bob," Miss Finney said. She reached into her shopping bag and took out some pieces of sugar. "You may feed him if you like."

Peggy put the sugar on her hand and held her hand way out. When Bob took the sugar, Peggy laughed because it tickled her hand.

When they left Bob, Peggy stepped right up to Miss Finney and walked beside her.

"Now," Miss Finney said. "Here is a dime. I'm looking for a place to spend it. I want to buy a present for another one of my friends."

Peggy wondered who *this* friend could be. But she didn't ask.

Maybe it was a squirrel, she thought. But Miss Finney walked past four squirrels and didn't speak to any of them.

Maybe it was a dog. But Miss Finney didn't speak to any of the dogs they passed.

Then Miss Finney saw a Balloon Man. "That's what I'm looking for," she said, "a balloon. I think that would make a nice present."

Peggy wondered what kind of friend would like a balloon, but still she didn't ask.

"I don't know what color to get," said Miss Finney.

Peggy thought red was best, but she didn't say so out loud.

"I think I'd better let my friend pick a balloon for herself," Miss Finney said, and she held out the dime to Peggy. "Go ahead, Peggy," she said. "Pick out the one you like."

"Me?" Peggy said. "Is the balloon for *me*?"

Miss Finney smiled. "Yes, I *said* it was for a friend."

When Peggy and Miss Finney left the Balloon Man, Peggy was carrying a red balloon. She was walking beside Miss Finney, and she was talking to her. Pretty soon they were planning to go to the zoo together.

At the zoo they talked to a goat, and gave peanuts
to a monkey. And all the time Peggy and Miss Finney
talked to each other.

When Peggy got home at the end of the day, she told her mother she hadn't gone *around* the world, but she had gone all *over* it. "And I talked to lots of strangers," she said. "Only guess what?"

"What?" asked her mother.

"The strangers really were friends," Peggy said.

Her mother nodded. "That can happen."

"And guess which one I liked best," asked Peggy.

"Which one?"

Peggy laughed because it was such a surprise.

"Miss Finney," she said.

# Reading and Following Directions

When you read directions that you want to follow, you must read very carefully. Could you follow these directions for making a toy airplane?

First, get a clothespin that has a spring on it. Paint the clothespin whatever color you want your airplane to be. After the paint is dry, stick a pipe cleaner or a paper clip through the spring part of the clothespin.

Put a button over each end of the pipe cleaner or paper clip. Then bend back the ends of the cleaner or clip to hold the buttons in place. Now the buttons are the wheels of your airplane.

Next, make a propeller out of paper and put it
on the top of the clothespin, like this:

Then use thin, flat wood or cardboard to make
a long piece with rounded ends, like this:

When you pinch this in the middle between the
tight ends of the clothespin, your airplane will
have its wings.

Your airplane won't fly, but you can pretend.
Push it along a table-top runway!

Whenever you read directions, try to understand
clearly just what things you are to do and in what
order you are to do them.

# Sound of Water

The sound of water is:
Rain,
Lap,
Fold,
Slap,
Gurgle,
Splash,
Churn,
Crash,
Murmur,
Pour,
Ripple,
Roar,
Plunge,
Drip,
Spout,
Slip,
Sprinkle,
Flow,
Ice,
Snow.

Mary O'Neill

# THE LITTLE BOY'S SECRET

## by David L. Harrison

One day a little boy left school early because
he had a secret to tell his mother.  He was
in a hurry to get home so he took a short cut
through some woods where three terrible giants
lived.  He hadn't gone far before he met
one of them standing in the path.

**W**hen the giant saw the little boy, he looked down at him and roared, "What are you doing here? Don't you know whose woods these are?"

"I'm on my way home," answered the little boy. "I have a secret to tell my mother."

That made the giant quite angry. "Secret?" he roared. "What secret?"

"I can't tell you," said the little boy, "or it wouldn't be a secret anymore."

"Then I'm taking you to our castle!" said the giant. Reaching down, he picked up the little boy and plopped him into his shirt pocket.

Before long, the first giant met a second giant. "What's that in your pocket?" he asked the first giant.

"A boy," he answered. "Says he has a secret he won't tell us."

When the second giant heard that, he laughed. "Won't tell us, eh?" he chuckled. "Well, we'll just see about that! To the castle with him!"

The giants thumped on down the path.
In a short time they came to a huge stone castle
beside the muddy river.

At the door they met a third giant. "What's
in your pocket?" he asked the first giant.

"A boy," he answered.

"A boy!" chuckled the third giant. He
brought his huge eye close to the pocket and
looked in.

"Says he has a secret he won't tell us," said
the first giant.

When the third giant heard that, he laughed
a terrible laugh. "Won't tell us, eh?" he asked.
"Well, we'll just see about that! On the table
with him!"

The first giant took the little boy from his
pocket and set him on the kitchen table.
Then all three giants gathered around and
stared down at him.

The little boy looked up at the first giant.
He looked up at the second giant. He looked
up at the third giant.

"Well?" said the first giant.

"We're waiting," said the second giant.

"I'll count to three," said the third giant.
"One . . . two. . . ."

The little boy sighed a big sigh.

"Oh, all right," he said. "I suppose I can tell
you. But if I do, you must promise to let
me go."

"We promise," answered the giants. But they
all winked at one another and crossed their
fingers behind their backs because they didn't
really mean to let him go at all.

The little boy turned to the first giant.
"Bend down," he said. When the giant leaned
down, the little boy whispered into his ear.

### Will He Tell?

**W**hen the giant heard the secret, he leaped up from the table, his knees shaking. "Oh no!" he shouted. "That's terrible!" And he dashed from the castle, ran deep into the woods, and climbed to the top of a tall tree.

The second giant scowled at the little boy.

"What's wrong with him?" he asked.

"Never mind," said the little boy. "Just bend down."

When that giant leaned down, the little boy stood on tiptoe and whispered into his ear.

When the giant heard the secret, he leaped up so fast that he knocked his chair over. "How awful!" he roared. And he raced from the castle, ran over a hill, and crawled into the deepest, darkest cave he could find.

The third giant scowled a terrible scowl
at the little boy.

"What's wrong with them?" he asked.

"Never mind," said the little boy. "Just
bend down."

When the giant leaned down, the little boy
climbed onto a teacup and whispered
into his ear.

When that giant heard the secret, he jumped
up so fast that he almost knocked the table
over. "Help!" he cried. "Help!" And he fled
from the castle and dived headfirst
into the muddy river.

The castle door had been left open, and since the giants had promised the little boy that he could go, he walked on home.

He told his mother his secret, but she didn't yell and run away. She put him to bed and gave him some supper.

The next morning when the little boy woke up, he was covered from head to toe with bright red spots.

"Now I can tell everybody what my secret was," he said with a smile. "My secret was . . .

I'M GETTING THE MEASLES!"

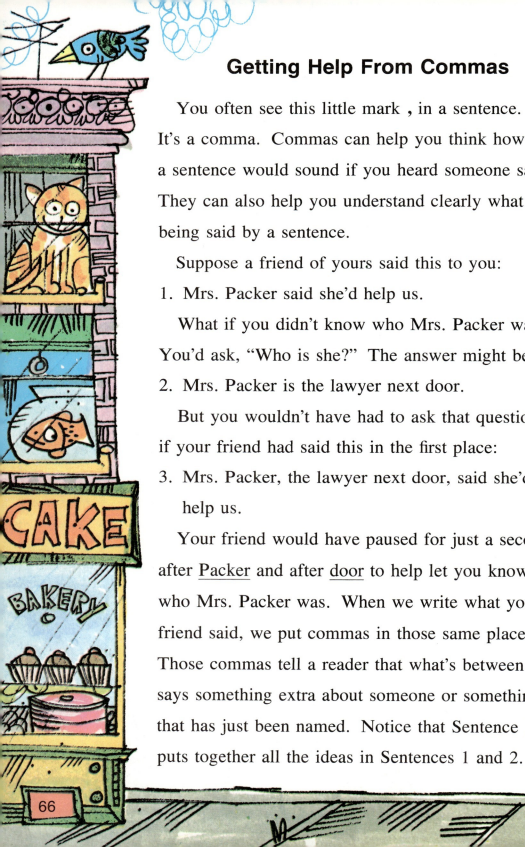

# Getting Help From Commas

You often see this little mark **,** in a sentence. It's a comma. Commas can help you think how a sentence would sound if you heard someone say it. They can also help you understand clearly what is being said by a sentence.

Suppose a friend of yours said this to you:

1. Mrs. Packer said she'd help us.

What if you didn't know who Mrs. Packer was? You'd ask, "Who is she?" The answer might be:

2. Mrs. Packer is the lawyer next door.

But you wouldn't have had to ask that question if your friend had said this in the first place:

3. Mrs. Packer, the lawyer next door, said she'd help us.

Your friend would have paused for just a second after <u>Packer</u> and after <u>door</u> to help let you know who Mrs. Packer was. When we write what your friend said, we put commas in those same places. Those commas tell a reader that what's between them says something extra about someone or something that has just been named. Notice that Sentence 3 puts together all the ideas in Sentences 1 and 2.

Now let's suppose that your friend was talking to Mrs. Packer instead of to you. Suppose your friend was telling Mrs. Packer that the lawyer next door had said she would help. Your friend might say the same words in the same order, but not quite the same way. The word <u>Packer</u> would be said in a little higher voice. The pause between <u>Packer</u> and <u>the</u> would be longer. And your friend wouldn't stop for even a second after the word <u>door</u>.

Here's how that sentence should look if we wrote it:

4. Mrs. Packer, the lawyer next door said she'd help us.

Notice that in both Sentences 3 and 4, each comma tells you to stop for a second. That stopping helps you know how the sentence would sound. Knowing how it would sound helps you understand the sentence. In Sentence 4, the one comma after <u>Packer</u> and no comma after <u>door</u> tell you that Mrs. Packer was the one being spoken to.

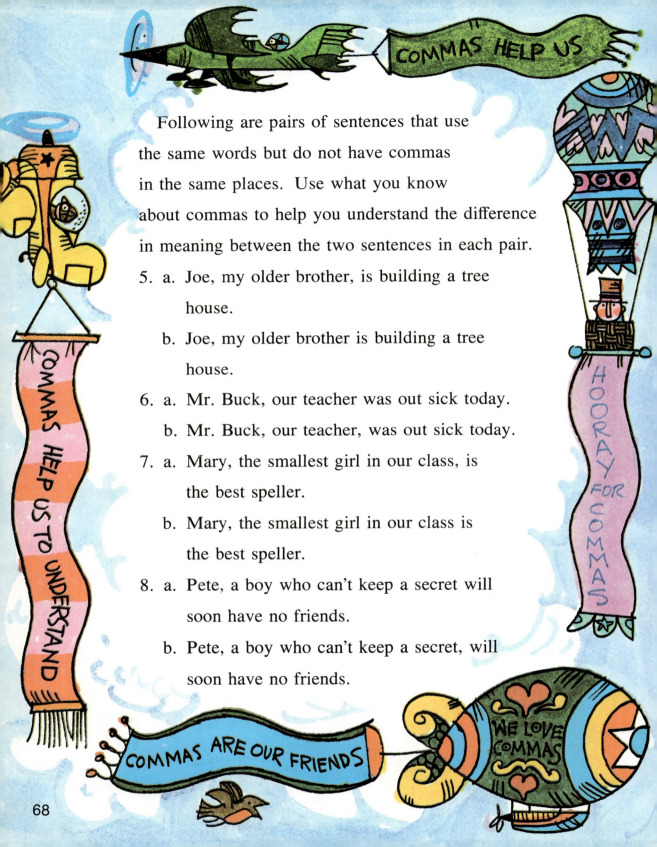

COMMAS HELP US

Following are pairs of sentences that use the same words but do not have commas in the same places. Use what you know about commas to help you understand the difference in meaning between the two sentences in each pair.

5. a. Joe, my older brother, is building a tree house.

   b. Joe, my older brother is building a tree house.

6. a. Mr. Buck, our teacher was out sick today.

   b. Mr. Buck, our teacher, was out sick today.

7. a. Mary, the smallest girl in our class, is the best speller.

   b. Mary, the smallest girl in our class is the best speller.

8. a. Pete, a boy who can't keep a secret will soon have no friends.

   b. Pete, a boy who can't keep a secret, will soon have no friends.

COMMAS HELP US TO UNDERSTAND

HOORAY FOR COMMAS

COMMAS ARE OUR FRIENDS

WE LOVE COMMAS

## Lyle

Tree won't pack his bag and go.
Tree won't go away.
In his first and favorite home
Tree shall stay and stay.

Once I liked a little home.
Then I liked another.
I've waved Good-bye to seven homes.
And so have Pops and Mother.

But tree may stay, so stout and straight,
And never have to move,
As I, as Pops, as Mother,
From land he learned to love.

**Gwendolyn Brooks**

69

# My Kitten

**by Aileen Fisher**

My kitten
has the softest fur,
as soft as silk to touch.
I smooth her,
and she starts to purr:
"Thank you very much."

And even
when I'm doing things
or when I want to play
she smoothes herself
on me and sings:
"Thank you, anyway."

# The Big Pile of Dirt

by Eleanor Clymer

On our street there was an empty lot. It was small, but it was full of junk. There was an old chair with the stuffing coming out. There were bottles and old tires and other things that people didn't want. And in the middle was a big pile of dirt. But I better not start telling you about that yet. First I will tell how we got started with the lot. It was like this.

See, we live in this old building. There's me. My name is Mike. I'm the oldest in my family. I have a sister Arleen, and two brothers, twins, five years old. Their names are Billy and Sam. After school Arleen minds them, when my mother is working. I have to help her sometimes when they act up.

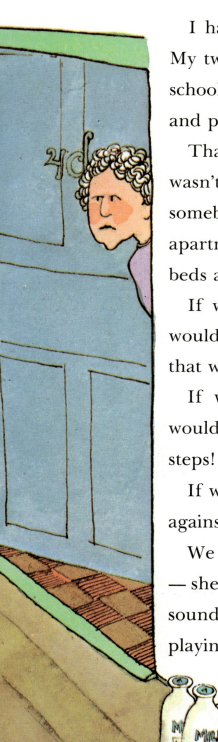

I have some friends that live in the building. My two best friends are Joe and Russ. We go to school together. After school we go some place and play.

That's where the trouble started. There wasn't anyplace to play. We couldn't all play in somebody's apartment. There's no room. The apartments have too much stuff in them — beds and things.

If we played ball in the street, the little kids would run out after the ball. They could get hurt that way.

If we played on the front steps, somebody would come out and say, "You kids get off the steps! You're blocking the door."

If we played handball, they said, "No handball against that wall."

We played in the upstairs hall. But Mrs. Casey — she lives in 4D — the minute she hears a sound, she pops her head out and says, "No playing ball in the hall."

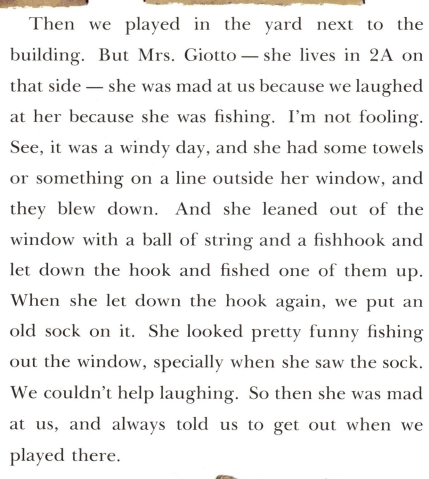

Then we played in the yard next to the building. But Mrs. Giotto — she lives in 2A on that side — she was mad at us because we laughed at her because she was fishing. I'm not fooling. See, it was a windy day, and she had some towels or something on a line outside her window, and they blew down. And she leaned out of the window with a ball of string and a fishhook and let down the hook and fished one of them up. When she let down the hook again, we put an old sock on it. She looked pretty funny fishing out the window, specially when she saw the sock. We couldn't help laughing. So then she was mad at us, and always told us to get out when we played there.

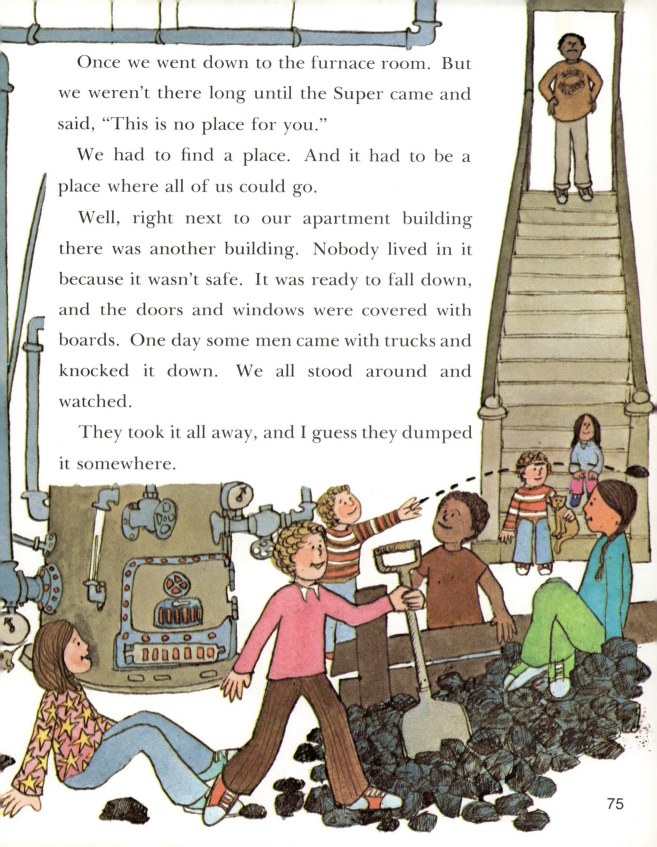

Once we went down to the furnace room. But we weren't there long until the Super came and said, "This is no place for you."

We had to find a place. And it had to be a place where all of us could go.

Well, right next to our apartment building there was another building. Nobody lived in it because it wasn't safe. It was ready to fall down, and the doors and windows were covered with boards. One day some men came with trucks and knocked it down. We all stood around and watched.

They took it all away, and I guess they dumped it somewhere.

Well, when they got through, there was nothing left but an empty lot with some bricks and old boards in it. Then it started to get full of junk. People would throw things in it, broken dishes and bottles and cans, and all the things people don't want.

Every day my friends and I would go and see what was there. We used to look for treasure, and we found some good things. I found a hammer that the men left. And Johnny was lucky. He found an old baby carriage with four good wheels. He used the wheels to make a racing car.

This was in summer, so we played there all day. We had to watch out for the little kids. Arleen had to be careful that the twins didn't get hurt with the broken glass and nails. Her friend Margie came with her little sister, and she would put things in her mouth if you didn't look out.

But still it was a pretty good place. We made a swing for the little kids out of an old tire. We hung it from some posts we drove in the ground.

And all the time we were waiting for somebody to tell us to get out, but nobody did. What happened was something else.

77

One day when we were playing, some ladies came. They came in a car with a man, and they all got out and stood looking at our lot. We watched them and heard what they said.

One lady said, "This is a mess. Look at all that broken glass and junk."

Another lady said, "This is no place for these children. They should be sent out of there."

A third lady said, "How can we have a beautiful city with places like this, Mr. Mayor? You must do something."

I thought to myself, "Could that be the Mayor?" And I got ready for him to chase us out.

But he didn't. He just said, "Yes, ladies, you are right. I will give orders for something to be done." Then they went away.

Joe said, "Now what? Will they make us get out?"

"No," I said, "they just want to clean it up."

Arleen said, "That means we get out. I knew it."

"Well, wait and see," I said. But I was afraid she was right.

But that is not what happened. Something different happened. One day a truck came. It was a very big truck, and it was full of dirt. Two men got out. They stood and looked at our empty lot. They scratched their heads.

One said, "Is this the place, Mac?"

The other said, "Yep. This is where we're supposed to deliver it."

So they backed the truck onto our lot, and dumped all that dirt right in the middle of the lot. Then they went away.

Russ asked me, "What's it all about?"

I said, "It beats me. I don't know."

We waited for something else to happen. But nothing happened. I went and stuck my hand in the dirt. It was nice and soft. It was clean dirt. It seemed like they wanted to give us a present. I thought we might as well enjoy it.

So I said, "Come on, kids."

Then we started playing. We climbed up the big pile of dirt, and slid back down to the bottom.

Then we started digging. We had no shovels but we got some pieces of board and some cans to dig with. The little kids were busy filling up old pots and dishes with dirt.

Some of the kids played supermarket. They put a board across some bricks for a counter. They filled up cans with dirt and made believe they were selling them.

You sure could do a lot of things with that dirt. We didn't go home until it got nearly dark.

The next day we went back. I was almost afraid to go. I thought the dirt would be gone. But it was there.

I had a great idea. I found a trash can cover. I climbed to the top and slid down. Pretty soon all the kids were sliding down.

My little brother Billy piled dirt inside an old tire. Then he got in and sat there. "This is my boat," he said, and he sat there for hours.

**Too Good to Be True**

One day Margie brought some flowers that she found in a trash can. She and Sam planted the flowers in the dirt, and Margie said, "This is going to be like a park. Don't pick the flowers."

Arleen said, "If it's a park, there should be benches for people to sit on while they mind the kids." So the girls made benches out of old boards. Joe and Russ and I had another idea. We dragged the old chair up to the top of the pile and took turns sitting in it. Someone had to keep an eye on things.

We kept waiting for something to happen to our pile of dirt, but nothing did. So we forgot. We just thought about it as if it was ours.

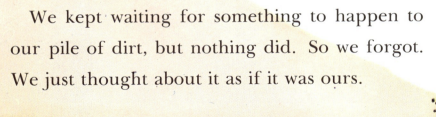

It got to be winter, and the dirt got hard as rock. We played we were mountain climbers. Then it snowed. It was great for sliding down. We built a snowman on top.

Then spring came and it got warm. One day Margie started to yell, "Look! Stuff is growing!"

We looked and there was green grass on one side of the pile of dirt.

Margie said, "Don't touch it, you kids. Keep off the grass." The kids took care not to step on Margie's grass.

Then Arleen said, "We should have trees." But where could we get trees?

One day Johnny found a can of paint. He painted trees on the wall of the building next to the lot. It looked good. It was almost too good to be true, which is what my mother says sometimes.

Well, one day when we were playing, a car stopped, and some ladies got out. A man was with them, the same Mayor.

We hid and watched. The ladies looked at our pile of dirt. One of them got mad.

She said, "Mr. Mayor, you promised to have this place cleaned up, but nothing has been done."

The Mayor said, "Yes, I remember. I gave orders to clean it up but somebody delivered a pile of dirt instead. Somebody else must still be waiting for that pile of dirt."

Another lady said, "Those children are still playing there. It should not be allowed. It is dangerous."

The Mayor said, "Yes, you are right. We will have it cleaned up and a fence put around it."

Joe whispered, "Are they going to take away our pile of dirt?"

Two little kids started to cry.

I said, "Keep still, you kids. Let me think." The ladies were pointing at our stuff and arguing. The Mayor kept shaking his head. I thought, "I have to do something."

Then before I could think any more, I marched out. I felt as if somebody was pushing me, only nobody was. I walked right in front of them and I said, "Excuse me, but please leave our stuff alone."

They all looked surprised. The Mayor said, "What's this? Who are you?"

I said, "I'm just one of the kids. This is our pile of dirt. We play here. Please don't take it away."

The Mayor said, "Is it all right if we look at it?"

I said, "Sure." So they went in the lot and looked at all the stuff we had there.

The Mayor said, "You see, children, we want to clean this place up."

I said, "We like it this way." I was awfully scared, talking like that to the Mayor. But I had to say it. I thought, "They are going to take it away from us, and there is nothing we can do. There is nobody to help us."

### Can Anyone Help?

But all of a sudden we heard a voice. "What is the matter? Did the kids do something?"

We all looked up and it was Mrs. Giotto, leaning out of her window. She said, "Wait, I'll be right down." In a minute she was down.

She said, "Those kids are not bothering anybody. You leave them alone."

I sure was surprised. She wasn't mad at us after all! The Mayor and the ladies were surprised, too.

One lady said, "But don't you see, this is dangerous?"

Mrs. Giotto said, "Nobody got hurt here yet. Those kids have no place to play. You should leave them alone."

Suddenly we heard another voice, "Yes, she's right. The children need a place to play." It was Mrs. Casey from 4D.

Then the Super came out. He said, "Since they have that dirt, they don't bother anybody. It's a good thing for them."

And suddenly I thought, "What do you know! They're on our side! They're fighting for us!"

The Mayor looked at us standing there. Then he looked at his ladies. And then he smiled all over his face.

He said, "You know what? I have a great idea. We'll make a park here for the kids."

Then all the grown-ups began to smile, too, and nod their heads, and Mrs. Giotto said, "Now you're talking."

The Mayor said, "We'll clean it up and put benches and swings and things to climb on. How would you like that, children?"

We stood there and couldn't say a word. It was too sudden. But Billy spoke up. He said, "What about our pile of dirt?"

The Mayor said, "Well, I don't know. It's hard to keep a pile of dirt clean. It gets all over everything."

Then I got brave and said, "We don't care. We like it." And all the other kids nodded their heads yes.

So the Mayor thought a while and then he said, "I tell you what. We'll move the pile of dirt over to one side and put some new dirt on. We'll build a little fence around it, and you can still have it. And we'll make a wading pool for you to wade and sail boats. How's that?"

It was our turn to think a while. Then Margie said, "What about the grass on the pile?" And Johnny said, "What about the painting on the wall?"

The Mayor said, "We could move the grass over, or we could give you some seeds to plant new grass. And we'll keep the painting. We could even give you more paint and you could paint the rest of the wall."

So we said okay.

Well, the next week the men got to work. They cleaned it all up. They had a bulldozer move the dirt into the back of the lot.

They built a pool, and they put benches and swings, just like they said. They put big pipes to crawl through, and big animals to climb on.

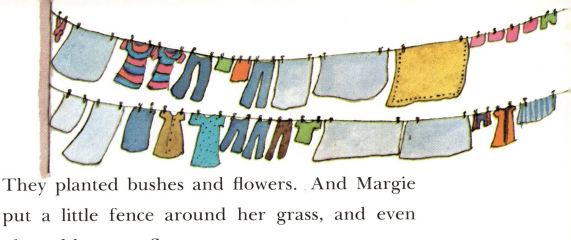

They planted bushes and flowers. And Margie
put a little fence around her grass, and even
planted her own flowers.

And we painted the walls. We made trees and
lions and mountains and all kinds of stuff.

It is a very good park, and everybody is proud of it. All the people on our block came to a party, and they take care of it and don't throw junk in the park. We sure needed that park.

But sometimes I go there by myself, real early in the morning, or when it has just rained, or in winter, because that's when there aren't so many other people around. And I make believe. I pretend it's the way it used to be, just a big pile of dirt in the middle of an empty lot.

WISHES AND DREAMS

# Wishes and Dreams

# BASCOMBE

## *THE FASTEST HOUND ALIVE*

by George Goodman

Once there was a farmhouse by a country
road.  It had a big back porch.  On the lowest
step of this porch lived a basset hound.

He had very long ears, so long they drooped on the ground most of the time. He had short stubby legs that were bent like horseshoes.

His name was Bascombe and he belonged to Mr. Winston.

At night he slept in the kitchen, and sometimes he ate there. But most of the day he lay on the bottom step and slept.

If anyone called him, he opened one eye just
the tiniest bit. Every once in a while a
caterpillar walked across his nose, and then
he opened both eyes. But he closed them
again, once the caterpillar was safely across.

One day two rabbits named Herbert and
Sam came by. They had just had lunch
in the garden, and now they were taking a stroll.
"Hi, Bascombe," said Herbert. "You look
sad. Are you sad about something?"

Bascombe's head slumped even lower,
and one of his ears drooped off the bottom step.
"Yup," he said. "I'm going to be sold."
"Sold!" said Sam. "Why, you're the best dog
around! You're the only dog that doesn't chase
us and lets us have a little lunch in peace."

"Why are you going to be sold?" Herbert asked.

Bascombe opened one eye just the tiniest bit. "Mr. Winston says I'm a hunting dog.  He wants to take me on the big hunt tomorrow, but I can't run fast enough."  Bascombe closed the one eye he had opened.

"Why, running is the easiest thing in the world," said Herbert. "Show him, Sam."

Sam ran off so fast that only the white of his tail could be seen.

"That Sam," said Herbert, "is the fastest
rabbit in this countryside.  Don't you wish you
could run that fast?"

Bascombe didn't even open his eyes.  "Nope,"
he said.

Sam returned a little out of breath.

"Bascombe," said Herbert.  "You don't want
to be sold, do you?"

"Nope," said Bascombe.

"Then you'll have to learn to run the way the other dogs do," said Herbert.

Bascombe sighed. He opened his eyes just the tiniest bit, and watched a caterpillar walk across his nose.

"We'll teach you how to run," said Sam. "Of course, you won't be able to run as fast as we can. But you'll be as fast as the other dogs and Mr. Winston will keep you. O.K.?"

Bascombe sighed again. "Yup," he said.

So they all went up the hill and down to the meadow.

"Now don't use up your breath sniffing and
yapping, the way the other dogs do," said
Herbert. "The real trick in going fast is
to wrinkle your nose like this."

And he wrinkled his nose.

"Then you spread your ears," said Sam,
"and give a big push with your hind legs."

Sam spread his ears and gave a big push
with his hind legs. And then he was out of sight
without really trying, because Sam was
the fastest rabbit in the countryside.

"Now you," said Herbert. Bascombe wrinkled
up his nose and pointed it. He spread his ears
and then he gave a big push with his hind legs.
Herbert blinked. All he could see of Bascombe
was a blur in the grass and a tail moving
very fast indeed.

Bascombe was really very good. In fact, he
caught up with Sam without much trouble at all.
"Now wasn't that easy?" said Sam.
"Yup," said Bascombe.
"And isn't it more fun than sleeping all day?"

"Nope," said Bascombe.

## The Hunt

The next morning Mr. Winston's neighbors came over with their dogs. There were fat dogs and thin dogs, tall dogs and small dogs, brown dogs and black dogs, and dogs that were all sort of mixed. They gathered around Bascombe.

"Are you coming with us? With those short stubby legs?" they asked.

"Yup," said Bascombe.

"Don't your ears get in the way?" they said.

"Nope," said Bascombe.

All the dogs put their noses to the ground and sniffed for a smell. Then they waved their tails in the air to show how eager they were. But Bascombe wasn't eager.

All this excitement seemed sillier and sillier. The dogs yapped and sniffed, and sniffed and yapped. Finally they got the smell.

Off they went, up the hill and down
toward the meadow, with Mr. Winston and all the
neighbors running behind. First came the tall
dogs, and then came the small dogs, and in
between were the dogs that were all sort
of mixed.

They were all yapping and sniffing and waving
their tails, all except Bascombe. He felt worse
and worse every minute, and he fell farther and
farther behind.

Suddenly he thought of a wonderful idea that
might take care of all his problems.  But he
would have to be the fastest hound of all
to make it work.

Bascombe wrinkled up his nose and pointed it.
He spread his ears.  Then he gave a big push
with his hind legs, and away he went.

He passed the small dogs and the dogs that
were all sort of mixed.  He passed the tall dogs.
He went so fast that all they could see was a blur
and the top of a tail moving very fast indeed.
The dogs were so surprised that they stopped
their sniffing and yapping and watched him go.

He went straight to the bushes, and out
of the bushes popped a rabbit.

"Bascombe found him!" cried the tall dogs.

"Follow Bascombe!" cried the small dogs.

"Do you see him, Bascombe?" cried the dogs that were all sort of mixed.

"Yup!" cried Bascombe.

He began to chase the rabbit. The rabbit ran across the meadow very fast, with Bascombe close behind.

Even the tallest dogs could hardly see the rabbit. All they could see of Bascombe was a blur and the top of a tail moving very fast indeed.

Some of the small dogs were already puffing. One or two of the smallest dogs were still sniffing at the bushes, for they had been too far behind to see what had happened.

All across the meadow the rabbit ran, until he got to his hole in the tree. He popped in.

### Sold?

"Mornin', Sam," said Herbert who was already there. "What seems to be the trouble?"

"A bunch of dogs have been chasing me," said Sam. "I'm the fastest rabbit in this countryside, but one of them is staying right on my tail."

"Impossible," said Herbert.

They both popped their heads out of the tree.

Coming across the meadow were some tall
dogs, and behind them, some other dogs, and
behind *them,* still sniffing and yapping, some
tired small dogs.

Way ahead of the whole pack, nose wrinkled,
ears spread, was — *"Bascombe!"* cried Herbert
and Sam together.

They both jumped out of the tree and
away they went back across the meadow,
with Bascombe close behind.

The small dogs stopped to rest.

"Who can keep up with Bascombe?" they said. "He doesn't sniff and yap, and he goes too fast. That Bascombe is the fastest hound alive. Let's go chase something slower somewhere else."

The small dogs turned around and went home.

Then the dogs that were all sort of mixed stopped.

"Who can keep up with Bascombe?" they said. "He goes too fast. That Bascombe is the fastest hound alive. Let's go chase something slower somewhere else."

Then the dogs that were all sort of mixed turned around and went home.

When the rabbits got back to the bushes, they ran right through. Bascombe followed close behind. Most of the other dogs ran around the bushes. The tallest dog of all tried to jump over them, but he landed right in the middle instead.

"That Bascombe," said the tallest dog, "is just about the fastest hound alive. Who can keep up with Bascombe?"

"We're tired," said the rest of the tall dogs. "Let's go chase something slower somewhere else." The tall dogs ran away, and even Mr. Winston and the other men went home with them.

Now Bascombe was the only one chasing the rabbits. They came around again and popped back into the hole in the tree.

Bascombe sat down outside. "Gotcha,"
he said, and he winked his left eye.

"It was your idea to teach him how to run,"
said Herbert to Sam. "Now we're trapped!"

"Bascombe, it's us," said Sam. "We taught
you how to run, remember?"

"Aw," said Bascombe, "I just ran fast to tire
out Mr. Winston. I didn't want to *catch* you."

All three of them looked across the meadow.
They could just see the last of the tall dogs
going home. Mr. Winston was going home, too.

"I don't care much for all this running," said
Bascombe. "I'm glad it's over."

After dinner that evening, Bascombe was
snoozing on the bottom step when Herbert
and Sam came by.

"I heard Mr. Winston say he was so tired
he'd never go hunting again," said Herbert.

"My idea," said Sam. "Wasn't it, Bascombe?"

"Nope," said Bascombe. "I thought that
part up."

"Now you can sleep all the time," said
Herbert.

"Yup," said Bascombe.

Many words end with common syllables like <u>ful</u> and <u>ly</u>. There are other common syllables that often come at the beginnings of words.

Look at the words in heavy black letters in these sentences:

1. She put a string of tiny, **round** balls **around** her neck.

2. The **head** of the ax flew off and hit the ground about ten feet **ahead** of him.

3. **Come** see this caterpillar that will someday **become** a butterfly.

4. He ran down that **side** of the street with a dog running **beside** him.

What was done to the first word in heavy black letters in each sentence to make the second?

The letters <u>a</u> and <u>be</u> are very often common syllables at the beginnings of words like <u>ahead</u> and <u>beside</u>. But not always! The letter <u>a</u> in <u>after</u> is not a common syllable. The first syllable in <u>after</u> is <u>af</u>. The <u>be</u> in <u>beak</u> is not a common syllable. The word <u>beak</u> has only one syllable because it has only one vowel sound in it.

When you meet new words that begin with <u>a</u> or <u>be</u>, it will often help you find out what those words are if you think the sounds those letters stand for in words like <u>around</u> and <u>become</u>.

Use those sounds now to find out what the words in heavy black letters are in these sentences:

5. He got a gold star as an **award** for jumping higher than anyone else.

6. What **amount** of money would you have if you had five nickels?

7. The hounds chased the rabbit **beyond** the gate.

8. Peanuts grow **beneath** the top of the ground, not above.

   Now look at the words in heavy black letters in these sentences:

9. Her **excuse** was that she got so **excited** she forgot to do what she said she would.

10. I hope she will **remember** to **return** my pocketbook.

Notice that the two words in heavy black letters in Sentence 9 begin with the letters <u>ex</u>. When those two letters come at the beginning of a word, they are always a common syllable and stand for the same sounds they stand for in <u>excuse</u> and <u>excited</u>.

Notice that the two words in heavy black letters in Sentence 10 begin with the letters re. When those two letters come at the beginning of a word, they are very often a common syllable and stand for the same sound they stand for in remember and reward. But not always! In ready and reaching, the letters re are only a part of the first syllable.

When you meet new words that begin with ex or re, it may help you find out what those words are if you think the sounds those letters stand for in excited and reward.

Use those sounds now to help you find out what the words in heavy black letters are in these sentences.

11. My brother **exchanges** stamps with another boy.

12. "Look out for that dog!" she **exclaimed.**

13. Everyone **expects** Sally to win the race.

14. Please **remain** after school to help with the books.

15. What kind of marks did you get on your **report** card?

16. How often do you **receive** a letter from her?

# SUNNING

Old Dog lay in the summer sun
Much too lazy to rise and run.
He flapped an ear
At a buzzing fly.
He winked a half opened
Sleepy eye.
He scratched himself
On an itching spot,
As he dozed on the porch
Where the sun was hot.
He whimpered a bit
From force of habit
While he lazily dreamed
Of chasing a rabbit.
But Old Dog happily lay in the sun
Much too lazy to rise and run.

*James S. Tippett*

# WHO'S IN HOLES?

The world is so full of a number of holes,
I'm sure we should all be as happy as moles.
There are holes all around
Made by chipmunks and gophers
And badgers and woodchucks —
All workers, no loafers;
Made also by prairie dogs,
Earthworms, and rabbits,
And others with similar hole-making habits.

Having no shovels,
No picks,
And no pails,
They dig with their noses
And dig with their nails.
They dig with their paws
And their claws
And their teeth
Till they've tunnels and rooms
Where they live underneath.
The earth is their floor
And their walls and their ceiling.
To be safe down inside
Is a wonderful feeling.

These holes are all sizes. They fit like a glove
The owner who enters the hole from above.
The hole of a gopher, for instance, you can't
Imagine, I'm sure, as the home of an ant.
The ant, the poor thing, would get lost almost always
And maybe catch cold in those long,
   drafty hallways.
Or think of a gopher
Attempting to enter
An anthole and pushing
His head in the center.

A hole has no windows
Narrow or wide,
For letting in light
And for looking outside.
But then, there's no scrape
And no rub
And no slosh,
For a home such as this
Has no windows to wash.
Besides, though it's true
That you haven't a view,
No passerby passing
Can peer in at you.
A hole makes a home that is private indeed,
The kind that at times almost all of us need.

Richard Armour

# Josefina February

**by Evaline Ness**

Not long ago on a high hill in Haiti there
lived a little girl named Josefina February.
Josefina lived with her grandfather,
Mr. February, in a house that had one room,
bamboo walls, and a banana leaf roof.

In front of their house stood a huge tree
in which Josefina had her private sitting room.
From her room in the tree she could watch the
sea a mile away, and the market place which
was halfway to the sea.

In back of their house was the grove.
In the grove there were oranges, breadfruit,
bananas, and yams. Lovely flowers grew
everywhere.

Early every morning Josefina and her
grandfather went to the grove and picked the
fruit which had ripened overnight. They carried
the fruit in baskets on their heads and walked
down the hill to the market place. With the
money they earned from the fruit they sold,
they bought candles, and matches, and other
things they needed at home. Mr. February
always gave Josefina a penny or two to spend
as she pleased.

Josefina loved the market place. There was
so much to see and smell and hear. People,
baskets, hats, and mats were all mixed in
with bananas and yams and sugar-cane candies.

There were bowls, necklaces, ribbons, and
shoes, and goats and oranges everywhere. Bells
rang, and children blew bamboo trumpets.

## Lost and Found

One morning, instead of going to market,
Mr. February went to work all day
in Mr. Hippolyte's sugar-cane fields. He told
Josefina to play at home — but Josefina
had other plans.

That day was her grandfather's birthday,
and Josefina wanted to buy him a pair of real
leather shoes. She decided to go to the market
alone. If she could sell one basket of fruit, she
would have enough money, with the pennies
she had saved, to buy the shoes.

After her grandfather left, Josefina took
the basket and went to the grove. While she
was picking the oranges, breadfruit, bananas,
and yams, she heard a strange sound. It
seemed to come from the berry bush. Josefina
looked behind the bush and saw a little black
burro. He had a fringe of brown hair
on top of his head that looked like a cap.
His legs were so wobbly he could hardly stand,
and his ears looked as long as his legs.

Josefina picked him up and held him close.
The little burro folded his soft ears and put
his head under Josefina's chin. She decided
to call him Cap.

She wondered if Cap belonged to someone.
How she wished he belonged to her! She
would teach him clever tricks. She would play
games with him. And when he was older, she
would ride on his back to the sea.

Josefina was so busy daydreaming, it was
noon before she remembered the fruit she had
picked to take to the market. She couldn't bear
the thought of leaving Cap, so she decided
to take him with her.

As she stood there in the noonday sun, Josefina suddenly felt cold. What if Cap belonged to the very first person she met? Would that be worse than the very last? First, last, last or first, it would be the same — if Cap belonged to someone else, he couldn't belong to her.

But perhaps he was like Josefina who had no mother, no father, no sister, no brother. Cap might not even have a grandfather. He might, just maybe, belong to no one in the whole world except Josefina!

Somehow she felt warmer, so she put her basket on her head, picked up Cap and started down the hill.

As she walked along, the first person she met was Lilly, the tallest, but not the friendliest, girl on the hill.

"Pardon me, Lilly," Josefina said. "As you can see, I have a baby burro here. Does he belong to you?"

Lilly swept by without a word.

When Lilly had gone, Josefina whispered to
Cap, "Well, anyway, it wasn't the *first* person."

She met no one else until she reached the
bottom of the hill.  There she saw a little girl
and her brother who were selling oranges
by the roadside.  Josefina went up to them
and said, "Pardon me.  As you can see, I have
a baby burro here.  What do you think of him?"

The girl and her brother, as if they were one,
said, "We wish he belonged to us!"

Josefina smiled and walked on along the
road.  Suddenly she heard a loud cackle, then
another, and another.  She turned around and
saw an old woman with three blackbirds. When
Josefina asked, "Pardon me, have you lost a
baby burro?" the old woman said not a word,
but the three blackbirds cackled, "Not we!
Not we!  Not we!"

Josefina felt light with happiness.  So far,
no one belonged to Cap!

Soon she came to a house that looked like a kite on a string. Two sisters named Yvette and Yvonne were standing on the porch. Josefina walked up to them and asked politely, "Miss Yvette and Miss Yvonne, would you know anyone who might have lost a baby burro? This burro here?"

Yvette and Yvonne smiled at Josefina and simply said, "No, dear."

Josefina hugged Cap and hurried on to the market place. When she got there, she could hardly believe her eyes. The market place was empty! All the people had taken the things they were selling and gone home to supper.

Josefina didn't know what to do. She was happy and sad at the same time. Now Cap belonged to her, but she had not sold the fruit and she had no real leather shoes to give to her grandfather for his birthday.

## The Birthday Surprise

She turned away from the market place and
started to walk slowly home. As she passed
Mr. Hippolyte's sugar-cane fields, she was
surprised to hear her name called. It was
Mr. Hippolyte himself leaning on the fence
with his big hat resting on his nose.

Josefina tried to smile, but instead she
started to cry. She wanted to tell Mr. Hippolyte
her terrible trouble, but right now she couldn't.
Mr. Hippolyte just waited. At last Josefina
blinked back her tears and told him her story.

Mr. Hippolyte looked at Josefina a long time.
Then he said, "It just happens that I have
a new pair of real leather shoes. Would you
be willing to trade Cap for the shoes?"

It was Josefina's turn to look at Mr. Hippolyte
a long time. Then she nodded her head and
very quietly said, "Yes."

While she waited for Mr. Hippolyte to return
with the shoes, Josefina took the ribbons
from her hair and tied them in Cap's mane.
She kissed Cap's nose and told him to be good.
She promised Cap she would never, never
forget him.

When Josefina got home, it was almost dark.
In a big pot she cooked ham and yams, and she
cut up all the fruit in her basket for dessert.
She had just put the shoes in the middle of
the table when Mr. February walked in. He
stood there and smiled at Josefina. And
Josefina stood there and smiled back. Then
Mr. February put on his real leather shoes and
kissed Josefina on top of her head.

Mr. February and Josefina sat silently eating
the birthday supper. They had almost finished
when Mr. February said, "Poor Mr. Hippolyte.
He has a responsibility, not a very big one.
But he thinks he cannot handle it alone.
He wondered if you would like to take care of it
for him."

Josefina stared at her grandfather.
Mr. Hippolyte had a responsibility! She started
to speak but before she could say a word,
the door slowly opened.

And in wobbled a little black burro, fringed
on top, with ribbons in his mane.

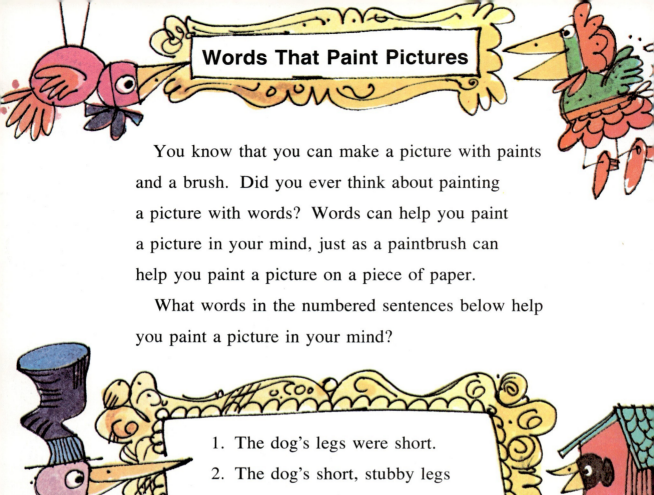

# Words That Paint Pictures

You know that you can make a picture with paints and a brush. Did you ever think about painting a picture with words? Words can help you paint a picture in your mind, just as a paintbrush can help you paint a picture on a piece of paper.

What words in the numbered sentences below help you paint a picture in your mind?

1. The dog's legs were short.
2. The dog's short, stubby legs were bent like horseshoes.

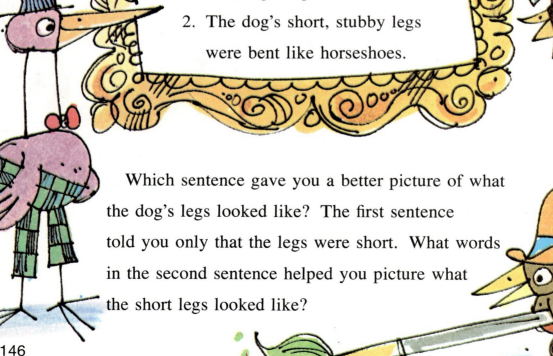

Which sentence gave you a better picture of what the dog's legs looked like? The first sentence told you only that the legs were short. What words in the second sentence helped you picture what the short legs looked like?

What words in the sentences that follow help you paint pictures in your mind?

The sun had been peeking between thin, white clouds when suddenly a black cloud filled the sky, and it looked as if it would soon be nighttime. Then great drops of rain poured down. Umbrellas of all colors began to cover the heads of the people hurrying along the sidewalks. Then, almost as soon as it had started, the sudden rain was over. Everything seemed to shine in the bright, merry sunlight, and a blur of rainbow colors stretched across the clearing sky.

Did you paint pictures in your mind to show what those sentences tell about? Did one of your pictures show the sun with a few white clouds around it and a black cloud moving toward them?

147

Did you make another picture that showed people who were carrying umbrellas of many different colors to keep off the rain?

After the rain was over, the words helped you paint another picture in your mind. Can you tell what the picture looked like?

When you read a story, notice the words that help you picture in your mind what is happening in the story. Doing that will help you understand and enjoy the story.

# Making Music

Most people enjoy music. Almost everyone has had a chance to play an instrument at one time or another.

Maybe you have played one of these instruments. There are many other kinds of musical instruments. The pages that follow tell about some of them.

This boy is playing
a violin.

A violin has four strings.
It is played by drawing a long bow
across the strings. The violin is
only one of many instruments
that have strings.

Here are some others.

This instrument is called a trombone.

The word trombone means "big trumpet."
It is played by blowing into one end and moving
the long arm back and forth.

Here are some other
instruments like the trombone.

This instrument is called a clarinet.

The clarinet player blows into one end and presses his fingers over the holes and keys to make different sounds.

These instruments are played like the clarinet.

This girl is playing the drums.

Drums help keep the beat when many
instruments play together.

Drums come in many
different sizes.

When many people play musical instruments
together, that group is called an orchestra.
The leader of the orchestra uses a baton
to help everyone play at the right time.

With so many different instruments, the
orchestra can play many different kinds
of music.

# Evan's Corner

## by Elizabeth Starr Hill

Evan walked
home from school slowly.
He stopped in front of a pet shop.

In the window, a yellow bird sang to him from its golden cage.

"Yellow bird has its own cage," Evan thought. "*I* want a place of my own."

155

He walked on. A bright pink
flower in a window caught his eye.
"Flower has its own pot," he
thought. "Wish *I* had a place
of my own."

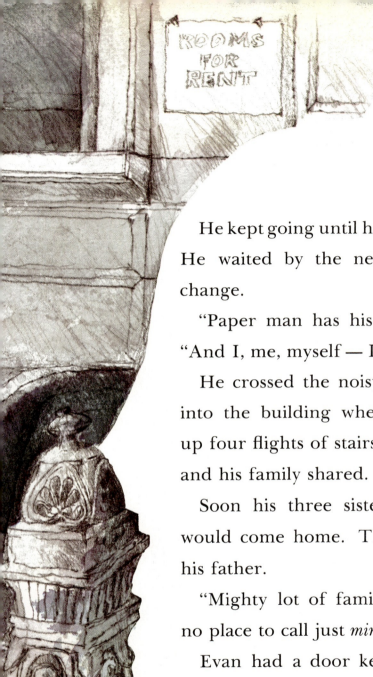

He kept going until he reached the big crossing. He waited by the newsstand for the light to change.

"Paper man has his own stand," he thought. "And I, me, myself — I need a place of my own."

He crossed the noisy, busy street and turned into the building where he lived. He climbed up four flights of stairs to the two rooms that he and his family shared.

Soon his three sisters and his two brothers would come home. Then his mother and then his father.

"Mighty lot of family," Evan thought. "And no place to call just *mine*."

Evan had a door key on a string around his neck so he could get in. Almost always he was the first one home. But today the door flew open before he even touched it.

"Surprise!" His mother stood laughing in the doorway. "I was let off from work early. Evan, I beat you home."

Evan gave his mother a big hug. He liked it when she got home ahead of him. Now they could have a talk by themselves before his brothers and sisters came in.

"Mama, you know what I've been wishing for *hard*?" Evan asked.

"Tell me." His mother smiled.

Evan told her the yellow bird had a cage. He told her the flower had a pot. He told her the paper man had a newsstand. He ended, "And *I* want a place of my own."

His mother thought and thought. At first it seemed she might not find a way.

But then her face lighted up. "Why, of course!" she said. "It'll work out just right. There are eight of us. That means each one of us can have a corner!"

Evan jumped to his feet and clapped his hands. "Can I choose mine?"

"Yes." She nodded. "Go ahead. You have first choice, Evan."

Evan ran to every corner of the rooms. One corner had a pretty edge of rug. Some had nothing much. One had a long crack in the wall.

But the one Evan liked best, the one he wanted for his own, had a nice small window and a bit of shiny floor.

"This is mine," Evan said happily. "This is my corner."

Evan's mother had no kitchen. She shared the kitchen down the hall with another lady. Often Evan went with her while she fixed supper.

But that night he didn't. He sat alone and happy on the floor in his corner.

His little brother Adam asked him, "Why you want a corner of your own, Evan?"

Evan thought for a minute. "I want a chance to be lonely," he said finally.

Adam went quietly away.

When supper was ready, Evan's father came to Evan's corner.

"Food's on the table," he said. "You want to eat with us, Evan?"

"Please, Pa," Evan asked, "if I bring my dish here, can I eat by myself?"

"Why, sure," his father said.

So Evan went and got his food and sat down on the floor again.

His family ate at the table in the next room. From his corner, Evan could see them and hear them talking and laughing.

When it was time for dessert, he joined them.

"Why, Evan," said his father, smiling, "I thought you wanted to eat by yourself."

Evan smiled back. "I was lonely," he said.

162

After supper, there were jobs to do. Evan helped clear the table. He brushed his teeth. He did his homework for school.

When it was done, he sat in his corner again and looked out the window.

The sky was almost dark. Two pigeons cooed sleepily on the window ledge. Stars lighted up, one by one. The breeze blew cooler.

Adam came behind Evan and said softly, "Are you being lonely now, Evan?"

"No," said Evan. "I'm just wasting time. In my own way. In my own corner."

"Can I ever come into your corner?" asked Adam.

"Why don't you choose a corner for your own?" said Evan.

So Adam did. He chose the corner across the room from Evan's. He sat in it. He called, "What will I do in my corner, Evan?"

"Whatever you like," answered Evan.

But Adam didn't know what to do. After a minute, he left his corner. He played horse with his big sister Lucy. He sat on her back and held onto her pigtails. "Gid-yup, Lucy-horse!" he shouted. They galloped round and round the room.

Evan watched the pigeons fall asleep on the ledge. He watched the sky get darker and the stars get brighter.

Finally his father called, "Come out of your corner, sleepyhead! It's time for bed."

Next morning, as soon as he woke up, Evan ran to his corner. His bit of shiny floor was as bright as ever. His window was still fun to look through.

But Evan felt that his corner needed something more.

What could it be?

163

He stared at the bare walls. "I know!" he thought suddenly. "I need me a picture! And I'll make it myself!"

In school that morning, Evan painted a picture of the sea. He drew big waves and a green boat.

He told his teacher, "I'm going to put this picture up in my own corner."

"That will be lovely, Evan," his teacher said.

When Evan got home, he hung the picture on the wall beside his window. After he had it good and straight, it looked just right.

Adam came home with their biggest sister, Gloria. She always picked him up at the day-care center on her way home from school.

Adam's eyes lighted up when he saw the picture. "That's mighty pretty, Evan," he said. "Do you think I could draw a picture for my corner?"

"Sure you could," said Evan.

Adam ran off. But he couldn't find any paper. He had no crayons. Lucy had, but she was busy with her homework, and he didn't dare speak to her.

He returned to Evan.

Evan was sitting with his back to the room and was looking up at his picture.

Adam asked softly, "Are you being lonely?"

"No."

"Are you wasting time in your own way?"

"No."

"Well, then, what *are* you doing?"

"Enjoying peace and quiet," Evan said.

Adam tiptoed off.

## What Evan Needs

That night, Evan didn't sleep well. He lay awake in bed, thinking about his corner.

It had a nice floor and a nice window and a nice picture. But was that enough?

"No," he decided finally. "I need something more. But what?"

He remembered the pink flower in its pot. He thought, "That's it! I need a plant of my own, in my own corner."

On Saturday, Evan went to the playground.
He took his toothbrush glass and a spoon.

The hardtop of the playground was cracked.
Grass and weeds grew up through the cracks.

Evan found a weed with big lacy flowers on it.
He dug it up with his spoon and planted it in his
toothbrush glass.

Then he took it home and put it on the window sill, in his own corner.

Adam came over to see what was going on. "What you doing, Evan?" he asked.

"Watching my plant grow," Evan told him.

"Maybe I'll have a plant, too, someday," Adam said softly.

Evan didn't answer. Something was bothering him.

Even now, his corner seemed not quite perfect. And he didn't know why.

"I got me no desk and no chair," he thought at last. "Why didn't I think of that before?"

Evan skipped off to the grocery store. He asked Mr. Meehan for two old wooden boxes.

"What do you want them for?" Mr. Meehan asked.

"Going to make me a desk and a chair," said Evan, "to put in a place of my own."

Mr. Meehan let him have the boxes.

In his corner, Evan stood one of the boxes up on end. Now it was like a high desk. He turned the other box upside down to make a bench. He sat on the bench.

Surely he had all anyone could wish for. And yet . . .

"How come I feel like something's still missing?" Evan wondered.

He puzzled and puzzled it over. Suddenly he remembered the yellow bird in its cage.

A great idea struck him. "I know!" he thought. "I need a pet to take care of. A pet of my own, in my own corner."

He ran to the pet shop.

He looked at the yellow bird. "Well, yellow bird," he thought, "you sing fine, but you're not the pet for me."

He walked into the store. A goldfish swam over to the edge of its bowl and stared at him.

"Afternoon, Mr. Fish," said Evan politely. But he thought, "No sir. That's not the pet for me."

He moved on to the turtle tank. A sign above it read: Turtle with Bowl, Only 50¢!

In the tank, about ten lively baby green turtles swam and scrambled all over each other.

One climbed up on a rock in the middle of the water. It looked at Evan. He felt like laughing. It must have been the funniest turtle in the world!

That baby turtle had a *very* thin neck. Its feet were big and homely. Its eyes were merry and black. If a turtle could smile, that turtle was smiling.

It took a dive off the rock. Clumsy turtle! It landed upside down in the water. Its legs waved wildly in the air.

Evan turned it over very carefully. The turtle winked at him as though it knew a secret. It looked as cheerful as ever.

"Yes, sir! Yes, sir!" Evan told that funny little turtle joyfully. "You're the pet for me."

Evan's heart beat hard and fast. He asked the pet-shop man, "Please, Mister, do you have a job a boy can do? I'd mighty much like to earn enough money to buy me a turtle."

"Sorry, son," said the pet-shop man. "I don't need help. Try next door."

Evan went next door. No luck. He crossed the street. He went from store to store asking for work. Still, no luck.

"Maybe some lady would pay me to carry her groceries," thought Evan.

He turned in at the supermarket. He stood just outside the check-out counter. A lady came through. "Carry your bags, lady?" Evan asked.

She didn't answer. She simply walked right on by.

Evan waited for the next lady. This time he smiled a great big smile and spoke a little louder. "Excuse me, but those bags look mighty heavy. Carry them for you?"

"Why, yes." She put them into his arms. "That would be a big help."

Evan carried the groceries up the block to where she lived. The lady thanked him. She gave him a dime.

A dime! He had a dime! Now all he needed was four more.

He raced back to the supermarket. He stood by the check-out. He waited. He smiled. He spoke politely.

Lots of ladies went past. But not one of them wanted him to help her.

Evan began to be afraid he'd never make another cent. Just then, a young girl said, "Oh, good! I hate carrying big bags."

She, too, gave Evan a dime.

"Only three more to go," he thought happily.

On Sunday, the supermarket was closed. But Evan went there right after school on Monday. He made one more dime, and then another. He had forty cents!

"Listen, you turtle!" he thought. "You're almost mine now."

But the next day, he fooled around for a while after school. When he finally got to the supermarket, a bigger boy was there ahead of him.

Evan's heart sank. He had supposed it would be easy to earn only one more dime. He stayed around all afternoon, hoping. But the other boy got the jobs. And Evan still had only forty cents. He began to fear that the turtle would be gone before he had earned enough to pay for it.

Next day Evan ran to the supermarket as fast as his legs would go. He ran right to the check-out counter. The other boy wasn't there!

"Hooray!" thought Evan. "Bet this is my lucky day!"

At first things were slow. Then, toward closing time, a great moment came. A white-haired lady said to him, "Sonny, do you think you could help me with this load of groceries?"

Evan said eagerly, "Yes, *ma'am!*"

Her bag was still on the counter. It was a huge one, filled clear up to the top. Somehow Evan got his arms around it and lifted it off the counter. "Where to, lady?" he asked.

"I live just next door," she said sweetly, "but it's three flights up."

Evan stumbled out of the store with the bag. He followed the lady next door without much trouble. But he thought he never *would* get up those stairs.

Yet at last he made it. Slowly and carefully, he set the bag down on the lady's kitchen table.

"Thank you," she said. Then she gave him the dime — the wonderful dime — the shining dime that made five!

Evan ran to the pet shop at top speed. He put the dimes on the counter and said proudly, "I earned some money, Mister! I'd like to buy me a turtle."

The pet-shop man counted the dimes. "All right, son. Pick one out," he said.

Evan looked into the tank. There were six turtles left. His eyes passed quickly from one green turtle to another.

Suddenly he saw a thin neck stretch up from the water. A turtle climbed up the rock — and fell off upside down, on his back.

"This one!" Evan picked the turtle up. "This one is mine!"

Evan carried the turtle home in a small bowl. He put it on top of the upturned wooden box.

Adam was already home from the day-care center. "What you got now, Evan?" he asked excitedly.

"My own pet," Evan boasted, "to take care of in my own corner."

Adam wanted to get a closer look at the turtle, but he knew he wasn't supposed to go into Evan's corner.

"Do you think I could ever have a pet of my own?" he asked.

"Sure. When you're much, much older."

Adam went sadly away.

Now Evan had many things.

He had a place of his own. He could be lonely there. He could waste time if he liked. He could enjoy peace and quiet.

He had a fine picture to look at.

He had a bench of his own to sit on, by his own window. His plant was growing tall.

Best of all, he had a pet to love and take care of.

Evan spent time in his corner whenever he could. But — it was strange. He still wasn't happy.

"I must need something more," he thought. "But what?"

He asked his sisters. They didn't know.

He asked his brothers. They didn't know.

His father wasn't home yet. When his mother came home, Evan said, "Mama, I'm not happy in my corner. What do I need now?"

His mother put her head on one side. Together she and Evan stood off from the corner and looked at it. It was beautiful. They both saw that.

"Evan," his mother said finally, "maybe what you need is to leave your corner for a while."

"Why?" Evan asked.

"Well," she said slowly, "just fixing up your own corner isn't enough. Maybe you need to step out now and help somebody else."

Then she left him. He sat alone on his bench, thinking over what she had said.

Adam came in. "Are you enjoying peace and quiet, Evan?" he asked.

"No," said Evan.

"What *are* you doing, then?"

Slowly Evan said, "I'm planning to borrow Lucy's crayons."

"Why?"

"To help you draw a picture if you want to. I'm planning to help you fix up your corner so it's just the way you want it. I'm going to help you make it the best, the nicest, the very most wonderful corner in the whole world!"

A big smile spread over Adam's face — and over Evan's face, too.

They ran across the room together to work on Adam's corner.

# Turtles

If turtles hide within their shells
There is no way of knowing
Which is front and which is back
And which way which is going.

John Travers Moore

185

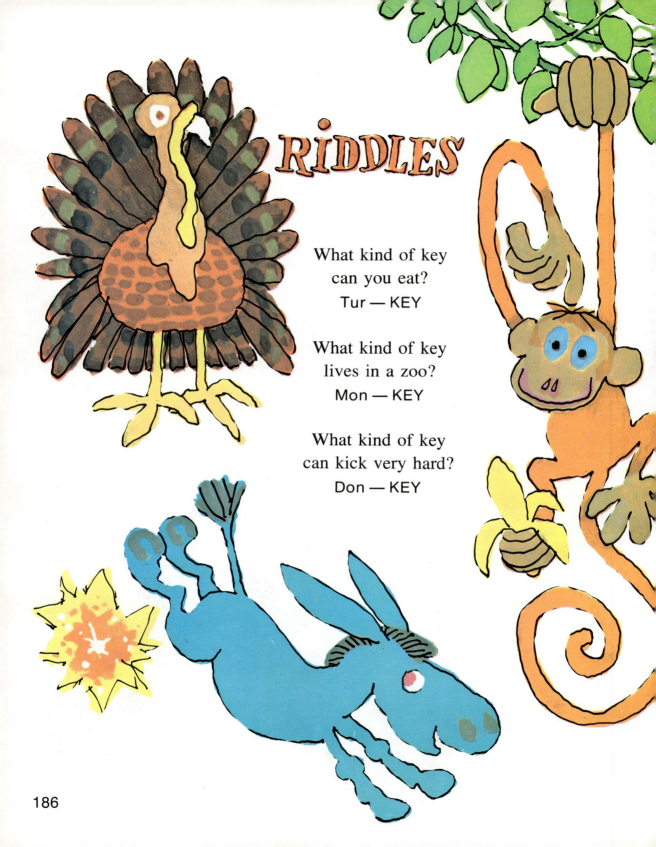

# RIDDLES

What kind of key
can you eat?
Tur — KEY

What kind of key
lives in a zoo?
Mon — KEY

What kind of key
can kick very hard?
Don — KEY

# PIP SQUEAK
## Mouse in Shining Armor

### by Robert Kraus

In all of mousedom, there never lived a braver
mouse than Pip Squeak, Mouse in Shining Armor.
Pip Squeak was the born enemy of dragonflies.
On his green toad, Hopper, he spent his days
riding from pond to pond chasing them. But
after a while, dragonflies were too easy and
Pip Squeak longed to fight a real dragon.

To pick up pointers, Pip Squeak watched the
seven knights who lived in the castle on the hill.
"You're a mighty small knight with mighty big ears,"
said Sir Prise, who was the head knight.

"I'm not a knight," said Pip Squeak. "I am a
mouse and my ears are just the right size."

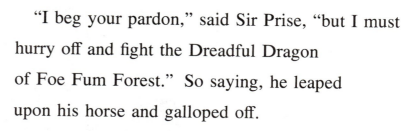

"I beg your pardon," said Sir Prise, "but I must
hurry off and fight the Dreadful Dragon
of Foe Fum Forest." So saying, he leaped
upon his horse and galloped off.

"Good luck," said Pip Squeak.

At sunset Sir Prise's horse returned without
Sir Prise. The six remaining knights were
quite upset. "Is there anything I can do to help?"
asked Pip Squeak.

"This is a job for a man, not a mouse," said
Sir Pose. "And since I am a man, it is up to me."
So he leaped upon his horse and galloped
into Foe Fum Forest.

"Good luck, for what it is worth," said
Pip Squeak.

Ten minutes later, Sir Pose's horse returned
without Sir Pose. "That was fast," said Pip Squeak.
The five remaining knights, whose names were
Sir Press, Sir Pass, Sir Port, Sir Plus, and
Sir Pent, said nothing.

"Maybe it is a job for five men," said Pip Squeak.

"That's an idea," said Sir Pass, and the five
knights leaped upon their horses and rode off
into Foe Fum Forest to face the Dreadful Dragon.

Ten minutes later, five horses returned without their knights. "Five are as fast as one!" said Pip Squeak, quite surprised. Now all seven knights were gone, and there was only Pip Squeak left to battle the dragon. He was sorry for the knights, but happy for the chance.

So Pip Squeak rode bravely out into Foe Fum Forest. "I just hope I don't come back without *you*," said Hopper.

"No more than I," said Pip Squeak.

He had not gone far when he came upon a witch.

"You are a very small knight with very large ears," said the witch.

"I am not a knight. I am a mouse," said Pip Squeak, "and my ears are just the right size."

"I beg your pardon," said the witch. "Your shining armor confused me. You are not going to fight the Dreadful Dragon of Foe Fum Forest, are you?"

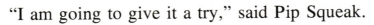

"I am going to give it a try," said Pip Squeak.

"I sell lucky charms to knights on their way to fight dragons," said the witch. "But in your case, I'm afraid I can promise nothing."

"That is quite all right," said Pip Squeak. "I don't need any luck for I have a bold heart. But thank you anyway."

"Everybody could use a little luck," said Hopper, as he pushed onward. The path was well-marked by signs which had been put there by the dragon himself, who feared no one and liked having visitors.

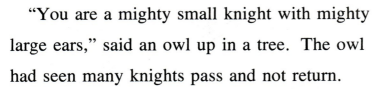

"You are a mighty small knight with mighty large ears," said an owl up in a tree. The owl had seen many knights pass and not return.

"I am not a knight," said Pip Squeak. "I am a mouse and my ears are just the right size."

"Knight or mouse, you are not going to fight the Dreadful Dragon of Foe Fum Forest, are you?" asked the owl.

"I sure am," said Pip Squeak.

"Do you think it is wise?" asked the owl.

"I don't know if it is wise," answered
Pip Squeak, "but it is certainly brave."

"What makes you think you can succeed when
everyone else has failed?" asked the owl.

"Every dragon has his weakness," said
Pip Squeak. "I have but to find it. That is how
I will succeed where so many have failed."

"That mouse not only has big ears, but he
also has a head on his shoulders," said the owl
as Pip Squeak and Hopper moved on.

## The Dreadful Dragon!

Suddenly Pip Squeak and Hopper were face to face with the Dreadful Dragon! He was indeed dreadful, and for a moment Pip Squeak almost lost his courage. But only for a moment.

"My, my!" said the dragon. "You are a mighty small knight with mighty big ears."

"I am not a knight," said Pip Squeak. "I am a mouse and my ears are just the right size."

"A MOUSE!" screamed the dragon. "The only creature in the world I fear!" — and he fled in terror.

"Well," said Pip Squeak, "this was really a job for a mouse after all."

"Hooray! Hooray!" shouted Hopper.

"Hooray! Hooray!" rang seven voices in the distance.

"That is either an echo or those are the seven knights whose horses returned without them," said Pip Squeak.

Pip Squeak followed his ears and there indeed,
tied to a tree, were the seven knights whose
horses returned without them. Pip Squeak leaped
from his toad and untied the knights, who began
to sing, "For he's a jolly good mouse."

Then Pip Squeak led the freed knights, singing
and cheering, back to the castle on the hill.
"I am sure your horses will be as glad to see you
as I am," said Pip Squeak.

For his boundless courage, Pip Squeak was made
an Honorary Knight of the Kitchen Table
in a special ceremony. "I dub thee Sir Pip Squeak,"
said Sir Prise.

Sir Pip Squeak's toad, Hopper, was given a special place in the stable alongside the horses of all the other knights.

"My dream has at last come true," said Pip Squeak. "Although now I am, indeed, a small knight with rather large ears."

# Spun Gold

# Spun Gold

## STORIES

## POEMS

## INFORMATIONAL ARTICLE

## SKILL LESSONS

# Fidelia
## by Ruth Adams

Fidelia Ortega belonged to a musical family.

Fidelia's father, Papa Julio, played the trumpet with a small band. The band played for weddings and dances and at the Mexican-American picnic that was held each year.

Fidelia's big brother Alberto played the trombone. He was in the school orchestra.

Fidelia's sister Carmela played the clarinet. She was in the school orchestra, too.

The orchestra played for school programs and P.T.A. meetings. Once a year the best players were chosen to be in the All City Orchestra.

Fidelia didn't play anything.

"You will have to wait," said Papa Julio. "I don't have the money to buy another instrument right now."

"You are too little," said Alberto. "Your arms are too short to work a trombone slide."

"You are too young," said Carmela. "You need all your front teeth to play the clarinet."

Fidelia did not care about any of that. She didn't want to play the trombone or the clarinet. She wanted to play a shiny brown violin.

"But you can't," said Alberto. "Your arms are too short, and your hands are too small. You could not draw the bow across the strings. You could not hold the strings down tight."

"You are just too young," said Carmela. "You are only in second grade. Miss Toomey chooses fourth graders to play the violin."

Fidelia thought, "I will talk to Miss Toomey."

So one morning Fidelia stopped by the music room and peeked around the door. The orchestra was practicing. Up and down went Miss Toomey's baton.

Fidelia could hear Alberto's trombone. She could hear Carmela's clarinet. And over them all she could hear the violins.

Fidelia tiptoed through the door so she could listen more closely. "How lovely!" she thought, as the violin bows swept across the strings.

Fidelia closed her eyes and took a step closer. *CRASH! BAM! BONG!* She stumbled right into a set of drums and sent them flying!

Miss Toomey lowered her baton. Everybody stopped playing and looked at Fidelia.

"Oh, no," moaned Carmela.

"Oh, no," echoed Alberto.

"What have we here?" asked Miss Toomey.

"It's our sister Fidelia," explained Carmela.

"She wants to play in the orchestra," said Alberto.

"Are you hurt, Fidelia?" asked Miss Toomey.

Fidelia shook her head.

"Come here and let me take a look at you," said Miss Toomey in a kind voice.

Fidelia walked slowly toward Miss Toomey. Miss Toomey leaned down to talk to her. "So you want to play in the orchestra?"

Fidelia nodded.

"What instrument do you want to play?" asked Miss Toomey.

"The violin," Fidelia whispered.

"You are a bit young to be a violinist," said Miss Toomey. "The violin is a hard instrument to play. However, we *do* need a tom-tom player for the Indian Dance we are learning. Would you like to try?"

Fidelia looked up. "Yes, I would," she said.

**Fidelia Has an Idea**

So Fidelia played the tom-tom with the orchestra. It was fun, but it wasn't the same as singing out a tune on a beautiful violin. Still, Fidelia did her best. She listened carefully to the music. She watched Miss Toomey's baton. She learned when to play more softly or more loudly. She learned to start on the downbeat and learned how to tell when to stop. But still Fidelia wished harder than ever that she could play a violin.

Every Monday Fidelia asked Miss Toomey if she had grown enough to play a violin. Every Monday Miss Toomey shook her head and said, "No, not yet, Fidelia."

Then one morning at orchestra practice, Miss Toomey said, "Boys and girls, Mrs. Reed is coming next week to choose the players for the All City Orchestra."

Everybody began to talk at once. *Tap! Tap! Tap!* Miss Toomey's baton called for order.

The orchestra began to practice the Indian Dance. Fidelia beat her tom-tom with a heavy heart. What could she play for Mrs. Reed? If only she had a violin. Then Fidelia had an idea.

On her way home from school, she stopped at the grocery store. "Do you have a small wooden box, with a lid?" she asked the lady behind the counter.

"Well, let's see," the lady answered. She reached under the counter. "Here we are. I thought there was one around somewhere."

"Oh, thank you," said Fidelia. She hugged the small wooden box and hurried home.

Down the block from Fidelia's house a new building was going up. Fidelia went to the lot and poked into a pile of boards there. At last she found a board that looked about right. "Please, may I have this board?" she asked one of the workers.

"Take the whole pile if you want it," the man answered.

"I just want this one board, thank you," said Fidelia.

Back home again, she took the box and the board into the garage and shut the door.

Fidelia took the hammer down from its place on the wall. She dumped a can full of old nails onto Papa Julio's workbench. Then she sorted through the tangled mix, picking out all the thinnest little nails. Now she was ready to begin.

*Tap-bonk!* Fidelia's first nail went through the lid of the box, but it missed the thin side piece.

She placed the next nail with more care.

*Tap, tap, tap.* There. The box was nailed shut.

She placed her board across the long way so that a good bit of it stuck out at one end.

*Tap-bonk! Tap-bonk! Tap-bonk!* "Ouch!" Fidelia stuck her thumb in her mouth. Then she took it out and shook it.

## Fidelia Gets Some Help

Just then Alberto came into the garage. "What are you doing?" he asked.

"I'm making something." Fidelia stopped shaking her thumb and stood in front of the workbench so Alberto couldn't see what she was doing.

"Let me see. Come on. I won't laugh." Alberto leaned over her shoulder.

Fidelia slid aside. "The nails won't go straight," she said.

Alberto picked up the box in one hand and the board in the other. He looked them over.

"What you need is a brace," he said.

Fidelia stared as Alberto pulled a large cardboard box out from under the workbench. On one side of it was written: ALBERTO ORTEGA — PRIVATE! Across the lid was written: KEEP OUT!

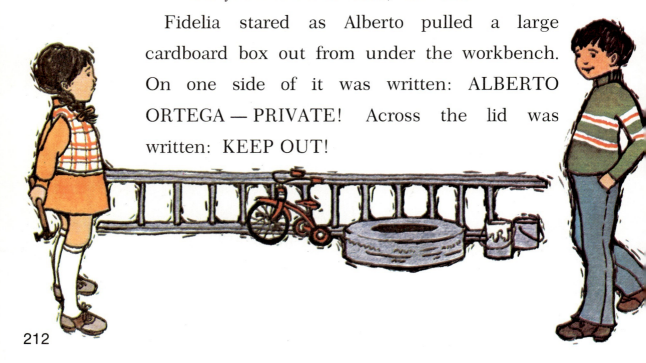

Alberto poked through the jumble in the box. He picked out three small blocks of wood. Then, carefully, he pried up the lid of Fidelia's small wooden box. He nailed one of the blocks of wood against each end. He placed the third one in the middle. A nail through the bottom held it in place.

*Tap! Tap! Tap!* The lid was nailed shut again.

"Now you have three braces to nail into," said Alberto.

"Okay, you hold the board," said Fidelia, "and I'll hammer."

Alberto held the board tightly to the box. Fidelia pounded a few good hard pounds. The nails went in straight, and the board was tightly fixed.

"That's great!" said Alberto. "What's next?"

"Strings," said Fidelia. "What can I use for strings and pegs?"

"Well, you could use rubber bands for the strings," said Alberto.

"That's a good idea," said Fidelia. "Carmela saves rubber bands on our door knob. Maybe she'll give me some. For pegs, I guess I'll just have to use nails."

Fidelia ran off to ask Carmela for some rubber bands.

"What kind do you need?" asked Carmela.

"Two fat ones and two thin ones, please," said Fidelia.

Carmela untangled four rubber bands from the rest. "Here," she said, "and here's another, in case one breaks."

"Thanks," said Fidelia, and she hurried back to the garage.

Alberto was pushing his box of junk back under the workbench. "Did you get the rubber bands?" he asked.

"Yes," Fidelia answered.

She picked up the hammer and nailed four nails at each end of the board. Then she stretched the rubber bands across the board and tied them in knots around the nails.

Fidelia plucked the rubber bands. *Twang, buzz, thwank.* "It sounds awful!" she cried.

"What's it supposed to be?" asked Carmela, who had come in to see what was going on. She looked over Alberto's shoulder. "If you're trying to make a violin, you need a bridge for the strings to go over. Wait a minute."

Carmela slipped out and returned with a clothespin. She slid it under the rubber bands. "Now try it," she said.

Fidelia placed the violin carefully under her chin and plucked away with the fingers of her right hand. With the fingers of her left hand, she pressed down on the rubber-band strings.

"That's pretty good for a homemade violin," said Alberto.

"It almost sounds like a tune," said Carmela.

"I wish I had a bow," said Fidelia.

"You can pretend a bow," said Alberto.

Fidelia sighed, "Yes, I can pretend a bow."

As Carmela and Alberto left the garage, Fidelia thanked them for helping her. She was glad they had gone — now she could practice in private. By dinner time the ends of her fingers hurt. But she knew exactly how to make the sounds she wanted.

After dinner, while the others did their homework at the kitchen table, Fidelia shut herself in the bedroom. When Carmela came in later, Fidelia was already snuggled into bed in the room they shared. The violin she had made was leaning against the dresser.

"Can't you make a tune yet?" asked Carmela.

"You'll see," said Fidelia.

**Try-out Day**

The day came for Mrs. Reed to choose the players for the All City Orchestra. Fidelia let Carmela and Alberto start to school ahead of her. As soon as they were out of sight, Fidelia put her violin in a big grocery bag.

She hurried down the street.

"I mustn't be late," she thought. But she slowed down as she came in sight of the school. In the parking lot was a blue station wagon. The back was packed full with music stands and instruments.

"That must be Mrs. Reed's car," she said to herself. Her heart began to thump.

The orchestra was tuning up when Fidelia
tiptoed through the door.

"Hurry up! We're going to play the Indian
Dance first. Mrs. Reed's already here," Carmela
whispered.

Fidelia leaned her grocery bag in the corner
and got the tom-tom.

She watched Miss Toomey. She counted
carefully. She played her very best.

After the Indian Dance, Mrs. Reed clapped and
said, "I see we are going to find many players
here for the All City Orchestra."

Miss Toomey said, "Next we will play a quiet
song."

That was what Fidelia had been waiting for. Carefully, and quietly she took her violin out of the bag. With loving care, she tucked it under her chin. When she heard the violins, she began to play. Fidelia knew just where to place her fingers to match the notes.

*Buzz ... Buzz ... zubb ... zubb ...!*

Miss Toomey tapped her baton on her music stand.

*Buzz ... Buzz ...* Suddenly Fidelia saw that everyone else had stopped playing. They were all looking at her.

"Oh, no," moaned Carmela.

"Not *here*," said Alberto.

Fidelia felt hot all over.

"Fidelia, come up here," said Miss Toomey.

Fidelia came.

"What is this?" asked Miss Toomey.

"It's a violin that I made," said Fidelia. "Alberto and Carmela helped me."

Mrs. Reed held out her hand. "May I see it?" she asked. She looked closely at the violin.

"Was this your own idea?" she asked.

"Yes," answered Fidelia.

"It was a good idea," said Mrs. Reed. "But I'm afraid you cannot play a tune on this violin — only pretend music."

"Oh, but I can play a tune," cried Fidelia. "I've been practicing. May I show you?"

Mrs. Reed smiled and nodded.

Fidelia carefully tucked the violin under her chin and began to pluck away at the rubber bands.

Sure enough, a good listener could hear the tune of "The Farmer in the Dell" among the twanging, buzzing rubber-band noises.

Mrs. Reed was a good listener. She watched closely, too. "Where did you learn the right way to hold a violin?" she asked when Fidelia had finished. "And how did you know where to place your fingers on the strings?"

"I watched the others," said Fidelia. "And I did what I heard Miss Toomey tell them to do."

"Would you like to play a real violin?" Mrs. Reed asked.

"Oh, yes! But I am too little and not old enough yet," said Fidelia.

"Hm," said Mrs. Reed. She walked over to Miss Toomey and spoke to her softly. Miss Toomey smiled and called to Alberto. Mrs. Reed handed Alberto her car keys and whispered in his ear. Alberto ran out the door. In two minutes he was back. Under his arm was the smallest violin case any of the children had ever seen.

Mrs. Reed opened the case. "This is a quarter-size violin, boys and girls. Let's see how it fits Fidelia."

It fit Fidelia exactly right.

She knew by the way her chin felt on the smooth black chin rest.

She knew by the way her arm bent neatly under the shining body of the violin exactly where it should.

She knew by the way her fingers curled over the fingerboard.

And she knew by the smiles worn by Miss Toomey and Mrs. Reed.

Most of all she knew by the smile in her own heart.

"Fidelia," said Mrs. Reed, "the boy who was using this violin needs a larger size now, so I am going to leave it here for you to use. Miss Toomey will start you in beginning string class. I will come back in a few weeks to see how you are getting along. How does that sound?"

"Wonderful!" exclaimed Fidelia. "Will I be able to play in the All City Orchestra?"

Mrs. Reed smiled. "Not this time," she said. "But if you do as well as I think you will, I'm sure you'll be in it within the next year or so."

Fidelia tucked the little violin under her chin. She set the bow on the strings. "I'm ready, Miss Toomey."

Miss Toomey put her arm around Fidelia's shoulders. "Beginning string class meets after lunch, Fidelia. Do you think you can wait until then?"

Two members of Fidelia's musical family were in the All City Orchestra. Alberto played his trombone and Carmela played her clarinet.

This year it was Fidelia's turn to sit in the audience and listen. But she didn't mind. She had a violin exactly her size, and she was in the beginning string class.

Everybody has to start somewhere.

# The Spring Wind

The summer wind
is soft and sweet
the winter wind is strong
the autumn wind is mischievous
and sweeps the leaves along.

The wind I love the best
comes gently after rain
smelling of spring and growing things
brushing the world with feathery wings
while everything glistens, and everything sings
in the spring wind
after the rain.

Charlotte Zolotow

# Finding Words in Alphabetical Lists

In a telephone book, people's last names are placed so that the first letters in those names come in the same order as they do in the alphabet. They are placed that way so that it will be easy for you to find someone's name quickly.

Sometimes the same thing is done with words. To find quickly a word that is in an alphabetical list, you will need to know the alphabet by heart and how to use it to find the word.

a b c d e f g h i j k l m n o p
q r s t u v w x y z

Suppose you came to the word <u>done</u> when you were looking for <u>hot</u> in an alphabetical list of words. Would you expect to find <u>hot</u> before <u>done</u> or after <u>done</u>? You should, of course, look farther on in the list because <u>h</u> comes after <u>d</u> in the alphabet.

Suppose you came to the word <u>kind</u> when you were looking for <u>hot</u> in an alphabetical list of words. Would you expect to find <u>hot</u> before <u>kind</u> or after <u>kind</u>? You should look at the words before <u>kind</u> in the list because <u>h</u> comes before <u>k</u> in the alphabet.

226

What if you came to a word that began with
the same letter as the word you were trying to find?
Suppose you saw <u>hurry</u> when you were looking for <u>hot</u>.
Now you have to think about the alphabetical order
of the second letters.  What are those letters
in <u>hot</u> and <u>hurry</u>?  Does <u>o</u> come before or after <u>u</u>
in the alphabet?  The word <u>hot</u> should come
before <u>hurry</u>, shouldn't it?

If a word you find begins with the same first two
letters as the one you're looking for, you'll have
to look at the third letters.  How do you know
that <u>hot</u> would come after <u>hope</u> but before <u>house</u>?
Why would <u>smell</u> come between <u>school</u> and <u>smile</u>?

Following are five words in heavy black letters.
Below each is an alphabetical list of four words.
Between which two of those four words would you
expect to find the word in heavy black letters?

| 1 | 2 | 3 | 4 | 5 |
|---|---|---|---|---|
| **quite** | **chair** | **sank** | **plant** | **wife** |
| class | candle | sail | people | west |
| love | clothes | safe | pinch | which |
| mess | cook | same | place | wild |
| thin | country | sat | play | wind |

# HAWAII

Hawaii is a chain of mountains standing in the sea. These mountains are called islands because of the deep water all around them.

Because Hawaii is made up of islands, its people are always close to the sea.

These mountains are made when pressure and heat build up inside the earth. Then melted rock shoots up through the earth's outer covering.

This jet of fiery rock is a volcano. When the huge pile of hot rock cools, it becomes an island.

Breakers are big waves from the sea which crash into the shore.

Water that cuts away from the sea into the land is called a bay. Even when the sea is choppy, boats are safe in the still water of the bay.

Hawaiians get many important things, like food, from the sea life around them. Many fish, sea turtles, and other animals live nearby in the clear blue water.

Plants grow well in the soil around volcanos. Hawaii is warm and sunny with more than enough rain.

Many bright flowers of all colors grow well on the islands. The people use these flowers to make the beautiful leis they wear.

The farmers on Hawaii can't grow many of the foods they need. But they do grow a few foods very well, and these are sold to lands across the sea. What food plants do you see growing here?

The roots of the banyan tree grow high in the air. They grow long enough to reach the ground. Then another tree begins to grow in the new place.

Hawaiian children love to swing on the long roots of the banyan tree.

Sliding down long hills on Ti leaves is muddy fun!

Hawaii is called a "melting pot" because its people come from many other countries and all live happily together.

# Ma Lien and the Magic Brush

## by Hisako Kimishima

There once lived in China a poor peasant boy named Ma Lien. Day after day he worked hard in the fields so that he would have food to eat and a small hut to live in.

Ma Lien's greatest dream was to be an artist, but the boy did not have even one coin with which to buy a brush.

One day as he stumbled along under a heavy load, he passed by the house of a famous artist. Going over to the gate in the high wall, Ma Lien peeked in, hoping to see the great man at work.

Silently he stood, watching the artist as he
painted a portrait of a mandarin. At last
the boy could hold his excitement no longer,
and he boldly spoke up.

"Oh, great one," he said, "could you let me
have one of your brushes — an old one that
you don't need anymore — so that I, too, might
paint a picture?"

On hearing this voice behind him, the artist
turned around. When he saw it was only
a poor peasant boy daring to ask for one
of his brushes, he became very angry.

"Ha, so you think you would like to paint!"
he cried. "Away with you and back to your
fields!" And he drove the frightened Ma Lien
from his gate.

But Ma Lien did not lose hope. He drew
pictures wherever he could, using a stone
to scratch on a flat rock, or his fingers to draw
in the wet sand of the riverbank.

When he returned to his hut at night,
he drew pictures on the wall by the light
of a candle. Soon he had covered the walls
with pictures of chickens, wolves, cows,
sheep, and everything he could think of.

With practice, Ma Lien became more and
more skillful.  But with all his skill, he still
did not have a brush.  One night as he lay
on his bed, he looked around his room
at all the pictures he had scratched
on the clay walls and sighed.

"Oh, if only I had a brush," he said. "What beautiful pictures I would paint."

With that, there was a flash of light, and standing before the boy was an old wizard.

"Ma Lien," he said in a creaky voice. "You have worked very hard and now you have earned a brush. Use it wisely, for it has great power." And saying this, he handed the boy a beautiful paintbrush.

Before Ma Lien even had a chance to say "thank you," the old man had vanished.

With a cry of joy the boy hurried over to the one bare spot on his wall and quickly painted a proud and happy rooster. But he had no sooner painted the last curling feather of the rooster's tail when the bird flew from the wall and landed on the window sill. There he gave a great *cock-a-doodle-doo* and flew off into the night.

"Now I know why the wizard said this brush had great power," said Ma Lien. "Do not worry, old man. I *will* use it wisely."

The next morning as Ma Lien was walking
to the mountain to gather firewood, he passed
a rice paddy. There he saw a man and a young
boy pulling a heavy plow.

Ma Lien quickly went over to the wall
of an old shed and painted a strong and
healthy water buffalo. Again, just as he
finished, the beast leaped from the wall
and with a low *mooo* headed down
to the rice paddy. Now with the help
of the buffalo, the man and his son soon
had the paddy ready for planting.

Just at that moment the mandarin came by.
Seeing the power of Ma Lien's magic brush,
he ordered his men to grab the poor boy
and bring him to the palace.

When they had brought Ma Lien
to the mandarin, he ordered the boy to paint
a pile of silver coins for him. Ma Lien,
remembering the wizard's words, refused.
The mandarin had him put into prison
with all his other prisoners.

Ma Lien soon discovered that the other
prisoners had done no wrong. The mandarin
had them put into prison so that he could
steal their lands. "Never fear," said the boy.
"I will have us all free before too long."

As the night passed, Ma Lien waited until
the guards had dozed off. Then quickly he
painted a door on the wall. The prisoners
pushed against it, the door swung open, and
they fled into the night.

The mandarin's men came chasing after
Ma Lien, but the boy easily escaped
on the fine horse he had painted for himself.

## The Mountain of Gold

Ma Lien knew he would not be safe if he remained on the mandarin's lands. So he rode for many miles until he came to a strange village. Here he kept on helping anyone he could with his magic brush. He painted buffaloes to help the farmers in their fields. He painted chickens for the farmers' wives, and he painted toys to keep the children happy.

One day he came upon some farmers hard at work carrying buckets of water to their dried-up fields. "That work is much too hard for you," said Ma Lien. And he set about painting a fine water wheel so that it would be easier to bring the water from the river into the fields.

And so it was that Ma Lien and
his wonderful brush became known
throughout the land.  It wasn't long before
the mandarin learned where Ma Lien was living.
He sent his soldiers to the village.  When they
found the boy, they grabbed him and
dragged him back to the palace.

The mandarin took away the brush at once
and ordered that the boy be put into prison.
"Without this I don't think he will escape so
easily," he chuckled.

Then he sent for the palace painter and
ordered him to paint a picture with the brush.

"What would you have me paint?" he asked.

"A tree," said the mandarin.  "A tree
with leaves of gold that will fall like the rain
when I shake the branches."

The artist went right to work and soon had
a fine tree painted on the wall of the palace.
But when the mandarin hurried over
to shake the tree, he got no more than a bump
on the head for his trouble.  The tree was
nothing but a painting on the wall.

Now the mandarin discovered that only
Ma Lien could paint pictures that would
become real. Sending for the boy, he spoke
kindly to him.

"Ma Lien," he said softly, "if you will paint
but one picture for me, I will set you free."

The boy, thinking of a way to trick the greedy
man, said that he would do as he was asked.

The mandarin's eyes lighted up with joy.
He handed the brush to Ma Lien and said,
"Paint me a mountain of gold."

The boy went to work at once, painting a big blue sea that spread all across the wall.

"Why do you paint the sea?" shouted the mandarin. "I ordered a mountain of gold."

"I have not finished," said the boy quietly. And with that, he painted a great gold mountain coming up out of the sea.

"Beautiful, beautiful!" cried the mandarin. "Now paint me a ship so that I can sail to my mountain and bring back the gold."

In a moment Ma Lien had painted a fine ship. The mandarin wasted no time in hurrying aboard with his finest soldiers. The sail was raised and slowly the ship rode out to sea.

"Too slow, too slow!" shouted the mandarin. "Give us a wind to speed us along."

Doing as he was ordered, Ma Lien painted a wind cloud. The wind came whistling down and the sails filled out. The wind swept across the water and made great waves around the ship.

"Too much!" cried the mandarin angrily.
"You will sink my ship." But Ma Lien paid
no attention. He went right on painting
storm clouds. Now the wind howled,
and huge waves crashed against the ship.
Then with a great *crrrack,* the ship split in two
and sank in the stormy waters.

Once more Ma Lien returned to his simple
life with the peasants, always ready to help
them with their work. And never again did
anyone ask him to use his magic brush
for evil and greed.

# RUFTY AND TUFTY

Rufty and Tufty were two little elves
 Who lived in a hollow oak tree.
They did all the cooking and cleaning
  themselves
 And often asked friends in to tea.

Rufty wore blue, and Tufty wore red,
 And each had a hat with a feather.
Their best party shoes they kept under the
  bed —
 They were made of magic green leather.

Rufty was clever and kept the accounts,
 But Tufty preferred to do cooking.
He could make a fine cake without weighing
  amounts —
 And eat it when no one was looking!

Isabell Hempseed

252

# Child of the Navajos

Seymour Reit

His name is Jerry Begay
and everyone calls him Jerry.
Jerry is a Navajo Indian boy.

Jerry is busily growing up in two worlds.
He is a typical American Boy. But he is also
a child of the Navajos. Woven into his life
are the modern ways of America
and the old ways of the Navajo people.

Jerry lives on the Navajo Indian Reservation
in Arizona. The reservation is spread out
over hundreds of miles.

Jerry lives there with his father, his mother,
and his little sister, Charlene.

This is Jerry's home. It is high up on Black Mesa.
A mesa is a mountain with a flattened top.
There are many mesas on the huge reservation.

Many Navajos make their living
by raising cattle and sheep. Jerry's
father owns many cattle, sheep, and
goats. Some of the cattle are grazing
near the house.

This is Jerry's school. It is called
Rough Rock School. The school is
like a little city, with its own water supply
and its own fire department.
Most of the children come from far away,
so they live at Rough Rock
from Monday to Friday. On weekends
the children return to their own homes.

Jerry is in the third grade. His teacher's name
is Miss Dodge. There are eighteen boys and girls
in Jerry's class. All are Navajos. Miss Dodge is
a Navajo, too.

Teacher and pupils speak and write
the Navajo language.

Here is a sentence in Navajo:

Shimá éí ajidiz dooleeł, diyogí jidootł'óół biniiyé.

Here is the same sentence in English:

My mother is busy spinning, so she can weave a rug.

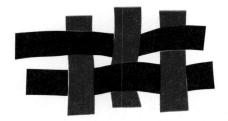

Now Jerry and his classmates are
beginning to learn English.
They are learning to speak English,
also to read and write it.

*floor*

Jerry and his classmates are also
learning arithmetic and art. Jerry
likes to draw pictures of his father's
sheep. "This one," he tells his friend
Louise, "is named Big Ears."

Everyone likes story-telling time.
Miss Dodge tells the children
some of the Navajo legends.
She sings Navajo songs for them.

From the older men, the children
learn Navajo dances. They learn
the Fire Dance and the Squaw Dance.
These dances have been done
by their tribe for hundreds of years.

At Rough Rock there are special School Mothers
and School Fathers. They live at school and
take the place of the children's real parents,
who are busy at home. Jerry's School Mother
sits with the boys and girls and helps them
with their meals.

She shows the children
how to make a special kind
of bread. It is called
fried bread because it is
fried in a pan.

School Mother shows the children how to spin wool with a spinning stick. She will use the wool to make a beautiful Navajo rug.

School Father tells the children stories of the past. He tells of times, long ago, when the Navajos were warriors and hunters.

When school is over for the day,
everyone hurries out to play.
"Come on!" Jerry shouts. "Let's have
a race to the playground!"

Later, after dinner,
School Father will come in
to say good night.

On Friday afternoon Jerry's father
comes to Rough Rock for him and
brings him home for the weekend.
For many years the family rode in
a wooden wagon pulled by a horse.
But now Jerry's father drives a new
pickup truck. Little by little
the old ways are changing.

### Jerry at Home

Jerry's sister, Charlene, isn't old enough to go to school yet. When Jerry comes home, she is always happy to see him.

A Navajo boy has lots of work to keep him busy. When Jerry is home, he helps to feed the cattle.

He helps to take care of the woolly sheep,
guarding them as they graze on the sagebrush
and pine branches and desert grass.
"Someday, maybe I will have sheep
of my own," he thinks.

At sunset, the sheep are
put inside a big wooden
pen. This keeps them
from straying at night.
It also keeps them safe
from hungry wolves.

Jerry's father must drive his truck five miles
to the well to get water for cooking and
drinking and washing. On weekends Jerry likes
to go with him and help to get the water.

Jerry's mother cooks
the family's meals
on a wood-burning stove.
Jerry helps to bring in wood
for the cooking fire.

When all the work is finished,
the family sits down to dinner.
Tonight Mother has fixed meat
and beans and fried bread.

On Saturdays,
Jerry often goes
to the supermarket
with his parents.
The family must drive
forty miles to get there.
Places are far apart
in Navajo country.

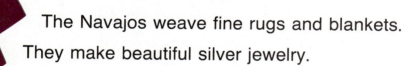

The Navajos weave fine rugs and blankets.
They make beautiful silver jewelry.

Jerry's uncle
is a silversmith.
He shows Jerry
how to cut and work
the shining silver.

"To be a good silversmith," says Jerry's uncle, "one must have the eye of a poet and the hand of an artist."

In the winter, Jerry's family lives
in a small, wooden house. But when
warm weather comes, the family
moves to another house called
a hogan. A hogan is made of hard
mud that covers a framework
of wood. The cooking fire is placed
in the middle of the dirt floor. Many
Navajo people live in hogans year
round. At one time, the Navajo
people all lived in hogans.

### Springtime

When spring comes to Black Mesa,
there are always new baby lambs.
Jerry's mother feeds the new lambs.
"Come along, little ones.
Time for your dinner."

Springtime is also picnic time.
On Sundays Jerry's family and their
friends go on outings. They go
to a place where there was once
an old Indian well. It is called
*To ha ha diee*, and it means,
"Place where the water is drawn."

After the picnic food
is eaten,
what can be
more fun
than to bump
and slide
down a sandy hill?

Sometimes Jerry goes off for a walk by himself.
He likes to climb the rocks and wander
among the piñon trees.

When he is by himself,
Jerry thinks about the people
of his tribe.

He remembers what grandfather
once told him — that the
Navajos will go on and on,
"as long as the rivers shall run
and the grass shall grow."

Sometimes, just for the fun of it, Jerry rolls
on the dusty ground and pretends that he's a
lively young calf.

And sometimes he likes to sit quietly
and think about himself.

Jerry wants very much to be a Navajo
like his father and his grandfather.
He knows that some day, like them,
he will be grown-up.

He knows that some day
he will do the Navajo dances
with the other men of his tribe.

This he knows, for he is an Indian boy.

This he knows, for he is Jerry Begay,
a citizen of America
and a child of the Navajos.

## More Help From Commas

You know that commas can help you understand what you're reading if you stop for just a moment whenever you come to one. You know from the commas that Sentences 1 and 2 below do not have the same meaning:

1. Mr. Hunter, our neighbor likes to fish.
2. Mr. Hunter, our neighbor, likes to fish.

Let's look at another way in which commas can help you understand what you read. Try to read this sentence:

3. At the picnic I had fried ham steak beans an apple pie some cheese crackers and peanuts.

How many different foods did that person eat?
Did the person have fried ham and steak, or fried
ham steak? Did the person have an apple pie and
cheese crackers, or an apple, pie, some cheese,
and crackers? You can't tell just what the person
had because commas were not put into that sentence
to show where the reader should stop for a moment.
In Sentences 4 and 5 below, commas have been put
into those sentences so that the same words say
things that are different.

4. At the picnic I had fried ham, steak,
   beans, an apple, pie, some cheese,
   crackers, and peanuts.
5. At the picnic I had fried ham steak,
   beans, an apple pie, some cheese crackers,
   and peanuts.

In Sentence 4, how many different foods were
named? How many in Sentence 5?

When you come to a list of things in your reading, notice the commas and use them to help you know exactly what the different things are.

Following are pairs of sentences that use the same words but have commas in different places. Use what you know about commas to help you understand the difference in meaning between the two sentences in each pair.

6. a. Margaret, Anne, Mary, Louise, Betty, Jo, and Susan are all coming to the party.

   b. Margaret Anne, Mary Louise, Betty Jo, and Susan are all coming to the party.

7. a. To wrap the presents, we need cardboard boxes, heavy string, paper clips, and ribbon.

   b. To wrap the presents, we need cardboard, boxes, heavy string, paper, clips, and ribbon.

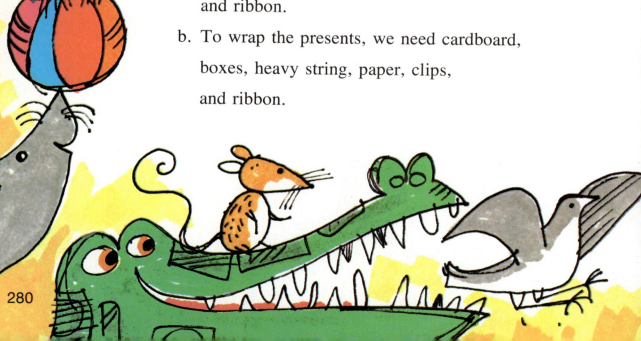

280

Use what you know about commas to help you answer the question below each sentence.

8. In my paint box, I have blue green, dandelion yellow, cream, white, and brick red.

How many colors are in the paint box?

9. a. Benjy, the boy who lives here, races pigeons.
   b. Benjy, the boy who lives here races pigeons.

Who is Benjy in the first sentence? Who is Benjy in the second sentence?

10. Into this box we'll put a spider on a string, a green frog, a stuffed lion, a toy tiger, and a grasshopper.

How many things are being put into the box?

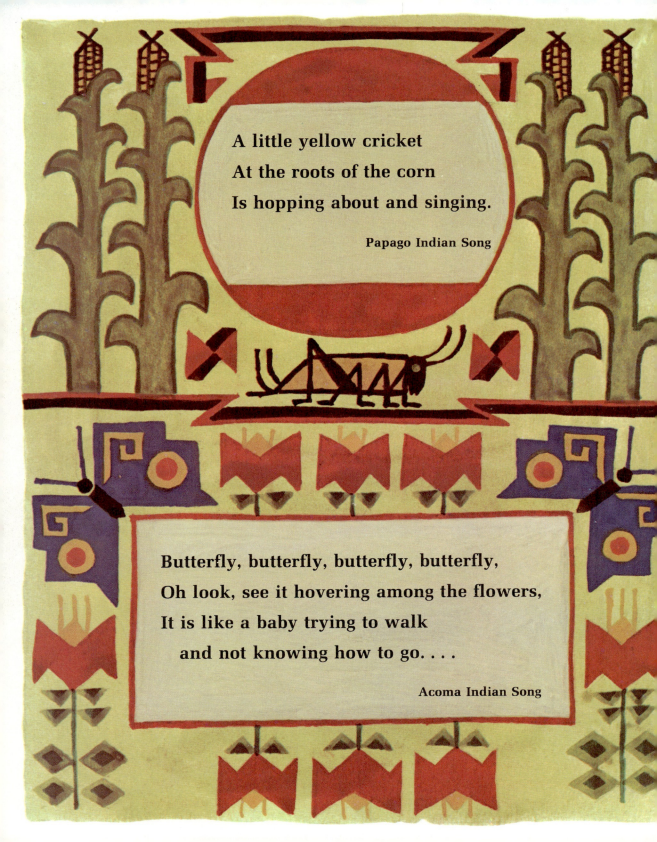

A little yellow cricket
At the roots of the corn
Is hopping about and singing.

Papago Indian Song

Butterfly, butterfly, butterfly, butterfly,
Oh look, see it hovering among the flowers,
It is like a baby trying to walk
and not knowing how to go. . . .

Acoma Indian Song

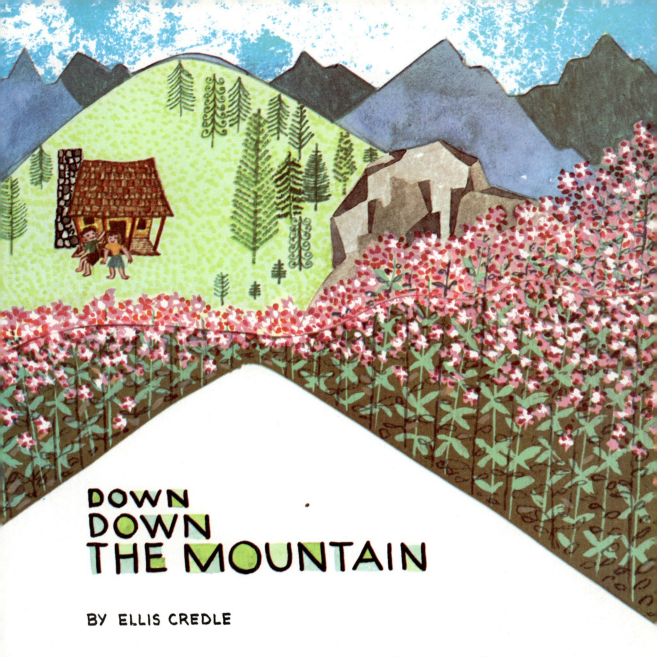

# DOWN DOWN THE MOUNTAIN

BY ELLIS CREDLE

Once upon a time, in a little log cabin up in the
Blue Ridge Mountains, there lived a little girl
named Hetty and her brother Hank.

Although their home was a small one, it was a cozy place to live. There was a big stone fireplace at one end. That was where Mammy cooked beans and pork in a big black pot. In the middle of the room, there was a long table made of boards. That was where Mammy and Pappy and Hetty and Hank ate their dinner every day.

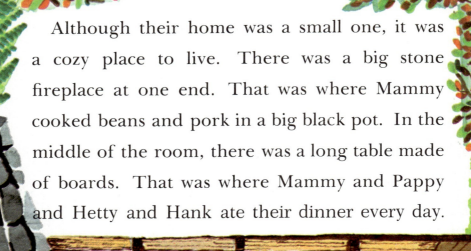

Never in all their lives had Hetty or Hank had a pair of shoes. In the summer it was fun to run around barefoot. But when winter came, their feet were very cold, and they longed for a pair of shoes.

They each wanted a beautiful shining pair that sang, "Creaky-squeaky-creaky-squeaky," every time they walked.

They begged their Mammy to buy them some shoes. She said, "You can't find shoes like that in these hills! Such shining shoes come from the town, away down down the mountain."

So they asked their Pappy, but he said, "There's not a cent of money in this house. We've everything we need right in these hills."

Hetty and Hank felt very sad, but they did not give up.

"Let's ask our Granny," said Hetty. And they did.

"Some shining shoes?" asked Granny. "I'll tell you how you can get them yourselves."

"How? How?" cried Hetty and Hank.

"Plant some turnip seeds," said Granny. "When they have grown into fine big turnips, you can take them down to town. You can trade them for some shining, creaky-squeaky shoes."

"Thanks, Granny. That's what we'll do," cried Hetty and Hank.

They raced away and planted some turnip seeds right next to Pappy's cornfield. Then they went home singing.

When Hetty and Hank got home, it was dark.
Mammy was waiting for them. She gave them a
nice supper. Then they went to bed. They
dreamed all night about shining shoes that
played a creaky, squeaky tune.

The next day they climbed up the steep, steep mountainside to see if the turnip seeds had come up. But they had not. Hetty and Hank had to wait and wait and wait before the baby turnip leaves peeped out of the ground.

Then there was plenty of work for Hetty and Hank! They had to pull the weeds each day, and chase away the worms, bugs, and grasshoppers that came for a taste of nice green turnip leaves.

When there was no rain, Hetty and Hank had to bring big buckets of water to make the turnip plants green again.

The little turnips grew and grew until they were the finest and the biggest turnips anywhere in the hill country.

Then Hetty and Hank brought Granny and Mammy and Pappy up to see them.

"Sakes alive!" cried Mammy. "I never saw such big turnips!"

"Yes, sir!" smiled Granny. "These are mighty juicy turnips."

"And they'll get a fine price in the town," said Pappy. "Hetty and Hank may have the old gray horse to take them down the mountain."

So Hank quickly brought the gray horse. Then they pulled up all the beautiful turnips and packed them into a big bag.

Pappy put the bag proudly across the gray horse's back. Then he helped Hetty and Hank up onto the horse. Now they were ready to go.

"Good-by!" cried Granny and Mammy and Pappy.

"Good-by!" waved Hetty and Hank. And away they went, clippety, cloppety, down the road to town.

# DOWN THE MOUNTAIN

They had not gone very far when they came
to an old man.

"Howdy, young ones!" he called. "What have
you in that big bag?"

"Some turnips we're taking to sell in the town,"
said Hank proudly.

"Oh, my! Turnips!" cried the old man. "How
I'd love some nice juicy turnips for my dinner.
Could you give me just a few?"

"I suppose we wouldn't miss just a few," said
Hetty, and she gave him some.

They rode on. After a while, they came to an
old woman who was making soup in a big black
pot.

"Howdy, children!" she called. "What have you
in that big bag?"

"Some turnips we're taking down to town," said
Hank.

"Turnips!" cried the old woman. "Deary me!
How I'd love just a taste of turnip for my dinner.
Couldn't you give me just two, for my husband
and me?"

294

"I suppose we wouldn't miss
just two," said Hetty,
and she gave the old woman
two big ones.

Down, down, down they went between the rows of tall blue mountains — down, down, down until they came to a little stream.

There the little road ended.

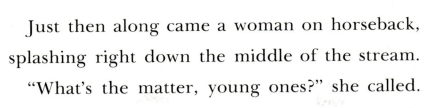

Just then along came a woman on horseback, splashing right down the middle of the stream.

"What's the matter, young ones?" she called.

"We've lost the little road to town," said Hank.

"Follow the stream," said the woman. "That's all the road there is in these parts."

So Hetty and Hank went splashing along and along. Pretty soon they saw the little road going up from the water.

They said good-by to the kind woman and gave her a bunch of turnips for her dinner.

After a while, they came to a man who was taking some turkeys down to town.

"Howdy," said the man. "What have you in that big bag?"

"Some turnips we're taking to sell in the town," said Hank.

"Turnips!" said the man. "I've had nothing to eat since sunup. What a treat a nice juicy turnip would be right now."

"We really should give him some of the turnips," said Hetty. And they did.

"Thank you, thank you," said the man. "You're good and kind young ones!"

Now they were very near to town. They could look down and see the rooftops in the valley. As the little road became smooth and straight, the gray horse broke into a gallop.

"Here's the town!" cried Hank.

Along they went, clippety clop, clippety clop, past the schoolhouse and past the little red store.

"Whoa!" cried Hank. "Here's the place to trade our turnips for some shining shoes!"

They climbed down and lifted off the bag. Somehow it felt very light and very empty. Had they given all their turnips away?

Hetty put her hand into the bag and brought out one large, fat, lonesome turnip. It was the only one left.

And there shining through the store window
were those beautiful, creaky, squeaky, shining
shoes!

Hetty and Hank looked at them longingly.
But one turnip would not buy a pair of shoes.

Two big tears began to roll down Hetty's
cheeks.

"There! There," said Hank. "No use crying. We'll just walk around and see the sights. Come on."

So they walked along the little road looking this way and that way. Along and along they went. After a while, they came to a field where there were many, many people. A big sign over the gate said "COUNTRY FAIR."

Hetty and Hank went hustling and bustling about in the crowd. Soon they came to a long row of tables with vegetables on them.

"Oh, here are some turnips!" cried Hetty.

"Are they as big as ours?" asked Hank.

Hetty held up her turnip. It seemed larger and juicier than the rest.

"Howdy, young ones," said the old man who was looking at the turnips. "Do you want to leave that turnip here for the contest?"

"What contest?" asked Hank.

"Why, there's a prize for the finest turnip at the fair," said the old man.

"Let's try it," said Hetty.

"Yes, let's," said Hank.

So the old man wrote their names on a card and tied it to the fat turnip. Then he placed it carefully among all the other turnips.

"You're just in time," he said. "I was just getting ready to judge the turnips."

He began to look carefully at the turnips. He felt each one to see how hard it was. He held each one to see how heavy it was. When he had tried them all, he held one large turnip high above his head.

"Folks!" he cried. "Here's the finest turnip at
the fair. It belongs to a little girl and a little
boy!"

Hetty and Hank listened carefully.

"Come here, young ones, and get your prize."

Hetty held out her hand, and there, shining
up at her, was a bright gold piece.

"Oh, thank you, sir!" cried Hetty and Hank.
"Now we can buy our shining shoes!"

They dashed past the beans and corn. They
dodged through the hustle and bustle of the
crowd. They raced along the street until they
came to the little red store.

The storekeeper was standing behind the counter.

"We want to buy some beautiful, creaky, squeaky shoes!" said Hank, all out of breath.

The storekeeper got down his brightest shoes, and Hetty and Hank each took a pair that played a creaky, squeaky tune.

Then they bought some presents to take home with them for Granny, Mammy, and Pappy.

Then off they started on the long trip home.
Up, up, up they went, round and round the
mountain.

After a long, long climb, they reached their own little cabin. There sat Mammy and Pappy and Granny waiting on the porch. How pleased they were to see Hetty and Hank and all the new things they had bought!

The next day was Sunday, so they put on their
beautiful things and went to the meeting house.

Hetty and Hank walked proudly into the
meeting house. Their shoes were playing such
a creaky, squeaky tune that all the people
stretched their necks to see who could be wearing
such beautiful shoes.